STOP WORKING START LIVING

I was having a crisis of Leadership.

My daughter was just about to be born.
My team's performance was through the floor.
I'd been knocked back from promotion not once but twice.

I hated where I worked and spent most of my time arguing with my managers.

The truth was, that behind all this – **I felt like I was a failure.**

To my wife, my unborn child and those in my care.

I felt unfulfilled in my work and my life. Clocking in, tuning out and going through the motion – day in and day out.

Something had to change, it needed to otherwise I was going to break. I had to find out who I was; the parent-to-be, the husband and most important the Leader I knew I needed to become.

I was starting to question what it is I truly wanted to contribute to the world and this book is the first parts of that journey to fulfilment - 'Purpose'.

For the last 8 years I've been doing the research on myself, on my colleagues and my clients helping to unearth 'Purpose'.

Now I know mine, it's vital I help others, in fact 100 million others in total.
This is the map.
These are the tools.
This is the way to move it forward.

Praise for Nathan and his book -

"This book feels like a casual chat with a man who has been through a lot and come out the other side. His advice is inspiring and compassionate. For years we've drummed the importance of purpose at work into employees. But for many, finding that is easier said than done. Most of us don't end up doing the job we dreamed of growing up, but this book will help us find our purpose whatever it is that we do."

- Gethin Nadin Bestselling HR author and Employee engagement expert

"Reading this book has opened my eyes to the rut I was in and in essence, thrown my world into a whirlwind; I can now see Possibilities where the only barrier is the limitations I set for myself, I can fully embrace my purpose and plan LIFE to the fullest.

I am in control of every aspect of my life and most importantly, I get to live life purposefully!"

- Didi H

"Having heard him speak, I now remember why I do what I do and realise actually I love my job"

- Liz, Teacher (expertise in Autism)

"Thanks to Nathan, I now feel more able and empowered to bring positive change to the world around me and more confident in my own abilities."

- Thomas

2

"He's knowledgable, fun and relevant. This was a fantastic session - very engaging. I could have spent all day listening to him.

Would be great to see him more often in the NHS."

- Anon feedback from training

"Nathan's a catalyst. He opens up your eyes, mind, and heart to accept your deepest goals. He helps you chart a path towards achieving them. His extensive knowledge in coaching and the business world are deep wells to draw upon and his wisdom invariably bears rich fruit when followed."

- Brandon

"Nathan shares with you his personal experiences combined with scientific theory and examples combined with stories of other well known individuals.

With the information and exercises that Nathan provides, helped me align myself to a future goal. It's worth the read. If you put in the work in his exercises, you'll understand Purpose and this just might help you get one step closer to Fulfillment!."

- Kevin

ISBN: 978-1-9163292-1-8 (Paperback)

Front cover image by Inc. Print
Book design by Inc. Print

First printing edition 2019.

Nathan Simmonds
Inc. Print

www.nathansimmondscoaching.com

CONTENTS -

STARTERS - THANK YOU'S AND GRATITUDE

Mum & Dad, for pushing me in ways you didn't understand. It was so great to be raised by you and to still be supported by you in all my ventures, no matter what path I decided to take at whatever point in my life.

My Big Brother, for pushing me in ways he's not ready to understand. You were the greatest role model of my life for what feels like a large portion of it, even if you didn't want to be.

My Bullies, for helping me see a world that only a victim could see from and giving me the experiences to share with others. You were, to me, horrendous people. You enabled me to hate myself. I dreamed about getting some sort of retribution. Then I realised what I'd been wasting my time doing and how it had held me back for so long. Now I get to see others do it and can help them make the decision faster to get on with life, not stay anchored to a bitter memory.

The people I bullied, I'm truly sorry. I'm also thankful for you being a part of my life and enabling me to see the other side of the table, again so I can share this with others. Jim, the only one I ever had a chance to apologise too face to face, thank you for your compassion and your understanding.

My friends, as well as the friends that stopped being friends. Everyone has been a lesson, a story, and an experience.

Anna, my girlfriend, for being just too good to be true. For challenging my thinking and introducing both of us to new ways of thinking. For encouraging each other to do bigger things, to travel, to see the world and create experiences.

Jay and Terry Brightwater, my spiritual guardians at a time when I truly needed you and for teaching me concepts that I have shared forward a million times. Thank you for your unerring grace and presence and curiosity no matter what was bought to your table.

Mestre Samara, my guide in the roda of life, how to be honest and say what you mean; integrity, flow and falling with style. Capoeira is the greatest way to learn how to fail and keep moving. *"You're either in or you're out. It cannot be half and half."*

Anna, my wife, firstly, for becoming my wife and not just my girlfriend. For keeping me grounded, for testing me, for being patient, for standing by me. For helping me keep my feet on the ground while I planned to make my moon shot. For helping challenge me to do things in different ways. For teaching me to communicate in a way to connect. Mostly, for being the person I trust most to hold the mirror up so I can see myself. I love you.

Poppy Grace Simmonds, my Daughter, compelling me to become the father, parent and leader I knew I needed to become. For pushing so many of my buttons, for helping me to reflect on how I enter into every conversation, for teaching me to teach patience even in the face of your deep 6 year old anger.

Simon Sinek   , writing '*Start With Why*', for turning up just as my daughter arrived and giving me a context with which to step into fatherhood. Your clarity of thinking has helped to craft how and what I do, it has helped me to help others focus on what they do and create deeper impact, get promoted, get pay rises and raise their own families in different ways. Thank you.

Dave Reynolds, '*Results Driven Training*'   for teaching and coaching me through my coaching qualification and constantly reminding me why I do what I do and why it means so much to me. Especially when we are in the throws of deep reflection about our work. Thank you for having the faith and encouraging me to go further.

Tim Ferris - For writing '4 *Hour Work Week*' and showing me there is another possibility, another path through and one that is doable in so many different ways.

Tom Bilyeu - Having watched so many interviews on '*Impact Theory*' I have seen the possibility and the potentiality in my thinking, with the mix of skills I have and can see the impact I am going to have on the world. The exposure here, on this show, has given me such an uplift in my thinking. Write things worth reading, do things worth getting interviewed by Tom Bilyeu for.

Peter Sage - My goal setting, ambition and mindset have never been quite the same. As a result, I continue to share these thoughts forward, combined with my own constant ripple creating that will reach a 100 million people - I don't know how, but, as you said the 'How' is none of my business.

Napoleon Hill – '*Think and Grow Rich*' Peter said to read your book, it was a great suggestion, with so much deep appreciation of great thinking. Thank you for doing what you did and the care and attention you poured into this.

Jamie Wheal and Steven Kotler – '*Stealing Fire*' You have opened my eyes so widely, and what is seen cannot be unseen. I've been able to reclassify my recreational experiences and direct them into the 0elevational. An immense combination of what I do with the infinite consciousness and all the possibility that goes with it!

Vishain Lakhani, '*Mind Valley*' - I have picked up so many vital learnings, and watched great teachers over and over, been inspired by the vastness of Mind Valley. So much so that it has inspired me to take action, to work to a level to not just be on your programs but to deliver as part of your program. Whether I make that or not is neither here nor there - it's the aspiration and the energy that matters.

Jade Andrews - For being a friend, a guinea pig, for listening, for learning and for doing so much with what I shared. Thanks for taking on board so much of it and taking yourself to a constant new level of thinking and approach. You've often said you wish you could do more for me, by doing what you do you give me everything you need to. That is such a huge motivation and inspiration

Tom Reeve - Thank you for your understanding, your enthusiasm and support. You have always been the technical wisdom and balance to that which I see in the emotional and in the people. You have turned that very effectively into numbers, results and faster played games. I have learned from watching you in how you have delivered those new skills, from me, to others.

Jamie Lewis - For wanting to learn, for helping me with getting ideas moving, for testing how I teach people, for challenging back. For resisting the lessons and finding out how smart he is when he implemented them. For being there as my sounding board when I needed to and for also questioning (at the right times)how big my ideas are which help me order them.

Bob Mckenzie, *'Benchmark for Business'* - for giving me an opportunity to shake Simon's hand. You've shown faith, support and care to be a mentor and a gift giver of the greatest heart. Thank you

Suzie Parkus - For being the communications teacher I always needed and for helping me network in the best possible way. For nudging me when my comm's were off and reminding me how far I've come, and how much I have achieved whilst bringing so many parts of my life together from the tangled web of pieces and disjointed thinking.

Parker Lazeski - For so politely sending an early draft of this book back and saying it needed more, because that was the impetus to take this book even further. Add the stories, add the understandings and add the humanity which you believed it needed.

fulfilment –
/fʊlˈfɪlmənt/
noun: fulfilment

1. **the achievement of something desired, promised, or predicted**.
"winning the championship was the fulfilment of a childhood dream"

2. **satisfaction or happiness as a result of fully developing one's potential**.
"she did not believe that marriage was the key to happiness and fulfilment"

3. **the meeting of a requirement, condition, or need**.
"the fulfilment of statutory requirements"

4. **the performance of a duty or role as required, pledged, or expected**.
"the need to eliminate excess by the security forces in fulfilment of their duties"

5. **Being 'Full' and being able to 'Fill' others**

THE ART OF FULL/FIL/MENT

"But, how the fu** do we get to that?"

The voice said, I sat and listened to it in my own head...

"Is it just me?"

"Why isn't anyone else saying they're not happy?"

"Everyone else is getting on with it"

"Must be me, I'll shut up then"

"I'll do as I'm told then"

"I just feel like sh**"

"This is sh**"

"What is the actual point..."

No, seriously, what is the actual point of it – not even just work, life as a whole?

Is it to commit 60% of my life to being unhappy in order to be comfortable later on in life when, most likely (for the majority), I'll not be in my physical prime to enjoy the free hours I have before I die?

Especially when the UK's retirement age continues to increase and average life expectancy finishes not that far after it.

Really?

F**k that. Every part of my being has been attempting to make sense of all of this for years now. And now I get it.

People are continuing to wonder why there's a subtle depression, sitting in the background, a quiet, tolerated depression related to and felt by 85% of the globally employed.

But, for some reason we do tolerate it. In fact, we learn to tolerate it from a very early age and have it programmed in and compounded over a period of time.

In physical terms, you don't sit on a drawing pin and accept it; you jump up and remove it. Yet, the slow drip of conformity in the work space builds steadily from the age of around 4 years old all the way through to either the moment you snap or the day you retire.

Even then, in the latter it still lingers on, with many retiree's professing the great industrial mechanisms. Work hard, grind it out, get a good pension. Build certainty, create security – in just the way they did inside the outdated framework. Yet, many feel lost with all the spare time gifted to them.

Life's different. We're different.

Have a look around, how many retirees do you know that just don't know what to do with themselves once they leave their job?

I found through my experience of work and this tolerance, that anxiety blends into depression. It steadily builds over time in the back ground. Neither is exclusive of the other, just a varying shade of the other.

Yet for extended periods of time you tolerate that element of doubt sitting at the back of the mind. We all do. I tolerated it for over 20 years.

A constant, but gentle, gnawing at the heart of things.

Persistent, yet not bad enough to go to a doctor for some pills and I doubt I ever would go to the doctors, not now. This is only possible because I know what the root cause is. I know that by doing what I'm doing I can move beyond it through the impact that I'm creating with and for others.

At some point though, we find out we have a problem, and I did. It starts, metaphorically, the moment you start balancing out the equation of taking the blue pill or the red pill. When you do this in your own head It's actually too late.

The moment you know there's an option and one of those is finding out how far down the rabbit hole you can go, you've actually already swallowed the 'red pill'. You're careening down the rabbit hole and there isn't any going back. Only a question of how fast and how deep.

"FOLLOW THE WHITE RABBIT" - TRINITY, THE MATRIX

What I'd learned so well through my journey, was to ignore the signs, the niggles and doubts. Then I started to question my own sanity.

Everyone else is ok, so it must just be me?

Or is it? Or is everyone else thinking something along the same lines and thinking they're the only one?

Is everyone staying quiet to avoid some learned reprimand that will happen if they suddenly pipe up?

I'm biased, that's for sure.

What I can say is I'd been doing this for a long time and I finally reached my breaking point and in my breaking down I broke out and broke through.

Sharing the idea's I've learned, the ones that have helped me succeed in reaching and accomplishing great goals. The ones that have pulled me through the hard challenges and the ideas that have built me up. Concepts that have been given to me and ones I've designed on the way to help support others learn the mechanisms to move faster.

The one thing I have been blessed with in some respect, since for almost as long as I can remember is that I have lived with the idea that *"There must be more than this"*.

I have constantly questioned *"What's the point?"* but more importantly have always known that I have a 'Purpose'.

This is why I have always felt challenged by certain jobs and felt the need to challenge other people's perspectives.

Especially when ethically and morally I and the work have not aligned. Yet on the flip side I have always felt that I'm meant to be doing something more important than this, something contributory.

Working and serving a cause rather than fulfilling someone else's agenda. Time and time again though, wandering and wondering from job to job seeking out some void in my life, trying to fill the perceived gap, but never truthfully knowing what that gap was.

While seeking to work out this gap and bridge it somehow, I've come to understand while looking out from my office chair, surrounded by co-workers; as animals we're not designed to sit in the same sedentary position all day.

Which most of us do on a daily basis while being pressurised to produce more, coerced into unhealthy competition to achieve someone else's target and never really having the opportunity to dig and dive into what truly drives us forward. This is where the frustrations begin.

It's the living up to someone else's expectation.

Doing what you feel you're obligated to do because that's what the education was all for.

Wasn't it?

We know the answer, truthfully, we do. Yet, we deny it constantly and the steady drip, drip, drip of expectation creeps up slowly and turns us into addicts and 'holics' of every kind.

Yet it's not kind, is it?

"ALCOHOL IS THE ANAESTHESIA BY WHICH WE ENDURE THE OPERATION OF LIFE."

GEORGE BERNARD SHAW -

But now, we have so many different modalities with which to endure.

We look for the mechanisms to help us deal with the thing we're doing. Everyone else is getting on and they're ok, mum and dad did it - so it must be me.

I must be the problem, wired incorrectly because I don't feel like I fit. I strived harder and faster looking for some sort of acknowledgment, recognition, or significance in what I did, yet was left feeling inadequate. It just never felt right.

The void seemed bigger than ever.

And as the void got bigger so did the 'things' I filled it with.

Like a parrot pulling its own feathers out when caged too long or an elephant grinding its own tusks off through inwardly pointed anger, we do what humans do best and self-medicate.

We get out of heads just to get out of our heads.

Whatever our drug or distraction of choice it's about numbing, distracting, smoothing the edges, enabling us to cope and deal with the perceived drudgery.

Legal, illegal, obvious, accepted or covert – it doesn't really matter. We do what we can to steal back some sanity, regardless of the consequences to ourselves and those around us.

I listened to some young boys full of bravado on the train journey home recently, 14/15-year old's bragging about how much Vodka they've drunk, how bad they'll feel in the morning and I wince.

I think about the blurred nights, the sexual encounters, the ruined relationships, the vast quantities of everything. The fights and all the toxicity that's piled up and I wish I could share even a little glimpse of it in order to help someone else make a better choice. Not to deny them the valuable lesson, to help them evolve from it faster.

It starts earlier than we imagine.

Regardless of the struggle, young or old - no one ever copes their way to incredible. No one.

What's the reason we do this? Dopamine.

EVERY DRUG HAS AN OUTCOME

That's all. Enough of a high to shut the buzzing in the ears down, drown out the sadness that sits in the background and enable you to keep plodding forward on Escher's square stair case pushing someone else's boulder.

Fu**.

Quite frankly that's a dark picture.

That's what it felt like at times when the purpose and meaning was missing from what I did.

The feeling though, because of the expectation, is then redirected to the quick hit dopamine. Rather than seeking out a healthy balance of all the brain chemicals, we flood just one to quench some strange thirst. We don't think about what the alternative jobs are.

We don't think about what we can do in the here, and now that will bring some joy, let alone more joy in the role. I did none of that at school or at work. I put my head down and pushed the boulder.

For me, my boulder pushing started when I was about 14. An energetic boy who learned through seeing and doing. My Father had spent hours with my brother and I. He taught us to build things, grow vegetables, cut, drill and nail shelves (ok my shelves aren't always straight) he gave us the fundamentals to work with and we still do.

Then I went to school, the seeing and doing was replaced with listen and repeat, this structure of systematic regurgitation just didn't work for me and I broke. The result; I was left feeling like Einstein proverbial fish being measured against its ability to climb a tree.

Then one day the bullying started. As I walked home 5 boys from another school nearer my home were walking towards me. I felt uncomfortable, I felt timid I knew something was coming.

"EVERYBODY IS A GENIUS. BUT IF YOU JUDGE A FISH BY ITS ABILITY TO CLIMB A TREE, IT WILL LIVE ITS WHOLE LIFE BELIEVING THAT IT IS STUPID."

- ALBERT EINSTEIN

The first day it was spitting and abuse. The next time it was a shove and the next it was a punch. I became the sport. I couldn't tell you how long this went on for, it felt like forever. Regardless of which way I walked, I obviously attracted them to walk the other way. It felt like every time they found me.

It felt like a life time – every walk home was terrifying, it was about finding the fastest route home to avoid being beaten up, spat on or verbally abused.

Between the system, with a teaching style that didn't suit me and physical repression I did the only thing I thought I could do; redirect my anger to everyone else.

I avoided dealing with the hurt I had by giving it to others. At school I became the bully, seemed like the natural thing to do. It fitted in with the 'hierarchy of pain' it never fixed anything I just proliferated it, perpetuated the cycle. The pain never left, I carried it forward, quietly. Occasionally it bubbled over, mostly I just forced the lid shut on it and kept it there.

What you never learn at that age is that your outer world is simply the reflection of the lessons you need to learn in your inner world in order to move beyond the current block. Until you learn those lessons, they'll repeat, and they did.

I learned to run home faster, take the longer route and never face up to that challenge. Now I know the lesson and I've learned huge parts of it already; forgiveness, compassion, challenge and curiosity.

Running faster or further doesn't teach you the valuable lesson, it just creates further distance from the solution that you're looking for. You have to stand on the brink sometimes, you have to face into the darkness regularly, you have to steer into the wind to see what it is you're made of.

Because, what I learned in retrospect, when you're standing there on the edge, physically and metaphorically, is that you can stop and you can have a look at what to do. You can work out where to go and what else you have to give. There is always something. There is always a truth in yourself to bring out.

As I continue to learn more about these experiences and how to better deal with them by improving myself inwardly, I have come to understand that you have to go and try out new experiences outwardly. Especially in these darkest moments, do the uncommon and sometimes the uncomfortable.

Experiences that enable courage in the face of adversity, that stimulate compassion, that deepen the learning about self and about others. You have to learn to put a smile on your face, not from a place of denial or naivety. One that gifts a smile to others whilst in search of your own meaning.

I didn't learn these things until much later, I managed to find more pain before I knew differently.

At 24 I had grown into a wiry man, more boy still trapped in a man's body. I exercised prolifically, pushing weights 5 times a week, martial arts 4 times a week. I had a high cut, close shaved mohawk style strip of dreadlocks pulled into a pony tail and tied with themselves. I vented large portions of my frustrations through exercise, but that wasn't enough.

Somewhere in that 24th year, I was lying on a dirty sofa, in a dirty terrace house about 20-minute walk from elephant and castle tube station. My arms pulled in tight to my body, my hands twisted inwards and tense like a praying mantis. My jaw juxtaposed to my face and my eyelids closed, unable to sleep.

Had you seen me you would have done 1 of 2 things; either pulled away in disgust at the mess I was or called an ambulance.

In simple, brutal terms - I'd overdosed on recreational drugs.

I'd taken 16 ecstasy pills and sniffed in excess of 5 grams of cocaine.

My only saving grace in this was that I'd been doing it for a while and my tolerance was high. Potentially anyone else going in at that level could have had catastrophic ramifications.

Now there will be people reading this and laughing, saying things like;

"Is that all?"

"What's he going on about?"

I used to say those sorts of things to. I used to encourage others to join me because misery loves company.

Actually, misery loves miserable company.

We only make those comments in order to bring others along for the ride, subtle collusion. We say it to make it look attractive and to lighten the mood of the damage being self-inflicted as a result of the unanswered questions gnawing at the back of the mind.

No one in their right mind puts themselves through that. If we are deeply happy or self-aware, we do not seek out toxic and damaging recreations to change our state.

"SO LET US THEN TRY TO CLIMB THE MOUNTAIN, NOT BY STEPPING ON WHAT IS BELOW US,

BUT TO PULL US UP AT WHAT IS ABOVE US, FOR MY PART AT THE STARS"

M.C. ESCHER -

ESCHER'S INFINITE STAIR CASE

Even Escher's stair case had an exit door. The lure was that the next flight would take you that bit higher.

It's an illusion, all of it.

You have a choice to keep going or get off and do something different.

Honestly, you do.

You also have a choice of how you see the journey.

Maybe it is a mechanism that enables you to do more good work in your spare time. Maybe it's the vehicle that pays you enough that once a week you volunteer for 'A Band of Brothers' and help young offenders rehabilitate.

Maybe it's the mechanism to build more strength to help someone with their stair climbing.

What if the stair climbing created enough space for you to willingly give 1 day a month for all your staff to go paint a local hospice? The pacing stops being monotonous. It changes dynamic.

When it becomes about what we bring, what makes us smile and how we give that to others, the game changes. Before this though, I starter to hear a quiet screaming waiting, wanting to be heard.

We have to listen to it. As Johan Hari shared;

"you need your sickness"

The screaming can become the sickness, it's a warning sign. You need it in order to propagate a new future. And that screaming is your voice, the one demanding to be heard, before being silenced through a self-perceived expectation that's been learned over a course of years.

If not listened to, it will break you.

"The world breaks everyone and afterward many are strong at the broken places. But those that will not break it kills. It kills the very good and the very gentle and the very brave impartially." – Ernest Hemmingway.

What needs to break, what needs to change, what do you really need to bring about?

JOHANN HARI -

"YOU NEED YOUR SICKNESS"

"THE WORLD BREAKS EVERYONE AND AFTERWARD MANY ARE STRONG AT THE BROKEN PLACES.

BUT THOSE THAT WILL NOT BREAK IT KILLS.

IT KILLS THE VERY GOOD AND THE VERY GENTLE AND THE VERY BRAVE IMPARTIALLY."

- ERNEST HEMMINGWAY

I broke several times, because I didn't pay enough attention, enough of the time. Then I started to and begun to evolve.
A latter boiling point; my failing sales performance. Turning into inappropriate outbursts at work, directed at poor leaders and ineffective departmental standards.

Yet nothing external to me changed as I continued to tirade and internally lament. Finally, with the arrival of my daughter I knew I had to changed, something had to change. Then, and only then, did I start asking questions again. More importantly I start asking myself higher quality questions.

Questioning myself with the view to improve.

Now 7 years later, my thinking is more fully engaged and I've written this book.

I've written this book from experience; it's not written about the pain point - it's written from the pain point.

As I typed these words, I worked 40-hours a week on someone else's agenda. I've worked in and helped multiple organisations whose ethics didn't aligned to mine, who's guiding principles, truthfully and in the majority, don't really focus on the people in their business or the clients they say they serve.

Up until then, I'd work inside the financial sector for 10 years. It's simply not about people it's about numbers – for many businesses in this space, whatever cost or price.

In part this book is my personal realisations coming to head, in having done over 20 years working like this; on other people's goals, because that's what I thought everyone else thought I 'should' be doing.

I've done the work that I was 'taught' to do and 'told' to do. I've pretended to do significant or 'meaningful' work in order to be able to tell others what to do.

As a result, I've spent my spare time numbing every emotion through almost every possible self-medication. I was stifled, confined and frustrated. Hiding the raw truth, I probably had depression* even though I did very well at covering it up. Or so I thought but not actually dealing with the truth that; I wasn't living up to my full potential or fullest expression and doing 'purposeful' work.

Purposeful Work is: 'Work' that, to me, impacts others and contributes to their growth and wellbeing.

I was afraid, shrink wrapped in the boundaries of my own comfort zone.

Thinking I was unable of achieving great things or realising great feats of accomplishment and as a result, I played small. I did this for far too long.

I write this from a place of my newer found truth. Not 'the truth', because no one can give you 'The Truth'

This is my version of it. The kind of truth that was always there, with the intention of helping others find theirs. That is what this book is for. Helping frustrated, ambitious leaders and professionals stop procrastinating, take action and do work that lights them up. It's about creating fulfilment and meaning in the work that we do. It's about how we create impact, find the deepest sense of satisfaction we can in what we're doing right now, and you can.

There is a way.

You can create an impact. One that reaches beyond what you've been taught to believe, one that extends beyond this current reality. You just have to start looking at the possibilities in a different way and shifting how you talk about those future facing thoughts.

This book is about you starting to find out what you're truly capable of, starting down the road of your peak potential. I have included some history and some elements of my journey, hopefully my realisation will give you a certain sense of clarity as you take your next steps at whatever level you're playing at. I also hope, through what I've achieved in my pursuits will
also demonstrate the possibility.

This book is about building a mindset that helps you to not be defined by your environment, it's about creating a consciousness that enables you to define your environment by what you decide to put into it – never wait for the stuff you think will make you to just happen.

Never wait and never chase the stuff you think you 'should' be doing. Be defining, creating and contributing.

The one thing you absolutely must chase is; your potential.
Be aware – your potential will expand in your pursuit of it. Enjoy the growth of it, not the perceived singular attainment of it, rather a growing sense of pleasure as you develop with it.

"IF YOU WANT TO FEEL HAPPY, DO SOMETHING FOR YOURSELF. IF YOU WANT TO FEEL FULFILLED, DO SOMETHING FOR SOMEONE ELSE."

SIMON SINEK -

* I say probably because I was never diagnosed and I never will be. I don't need to be. What I did to myself was enough to use this category of thinking.

Now I know what purposeful work really looks like. I understand the thrill and excitement of going home with a sense of pride at what I've contributed and how someone else's life will be changed for the better. How they can now positively impact other people they come into contact with.

When we are "on purpose", we are doing it for the greater good, we are doing it to connect - Life is a contact sport and we have to build our tribes so they can build theirs. We get to contribute in order that others can contribute at a higher level.
That's purposeful work at its essence.

What I have learned through Leadership and Coaching over more than 20 years; Purposeful work expresses itself differently through every individual, yet the outcome is still the same –
contribution leading to growth.

We can all tap into this sensation because purpose is a feeling we cultivate, not something that excludes us or eludes us.

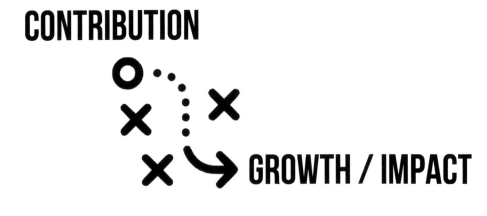

CONTRIBUTION

GROWTH / IMPACT

ABOUT THIS BOOK

I've prided myself on having the 'challenging' conversations with people, and I hope you find this book is much of the same, just on paper. If you're looking for the easy conversation or a short cut, I'm not that person. I maybe kind and considerate, but the questions and answer will remain the same.

There are no short cuts to becoming incredible. It takes time, execution and repetition. It's a process, and your brain may well say it's hard.

That 'Hard', that's the logical part of your brain doing itself best to protect you from pain. Pain is a good thing; you need it to create momentum.

Trust me, I know. It's the suffering that makes it difficult. I also know that part as well.

The best thing you can do is start early, the second-best thing you can do is start now – and if you have the luxury of starting early and doing something new now, then marvellous, crack on!

Most people come to me when there's a 'something' stopping them from stepping over barrier it or breaking through an obstacle. They want guidance to clarify the hindrance and better equip themselves mentally to overcome that which is holding them back.

Regardless if this is a niggle of doubt, or some level of uncertainty that has turned into procrastination. They know the answer is inside them but seem unable to find it. It's the voice of the critic perhaps holding them back.

Now maybe you've gotten bored of the sound of your inner doubt and the lack of action. Maybe you realized the questions you needed to ask and picked up this book. Now, you're right here, right now – Thank you! From me and from your future self, we both appreciate it.

In this book, you will find solutions that address the questions and gaps you are facing in creating fulfilment in your life right now with what you spend the majority of your life doing, help manifest your ideal future and develop a more impactful version of you.

How do I know? Because I have experienced everything I just described. As I said, I'm not writing this book about the pain point; I'm wrote it from the pain point. This book has been the natural consequence of years of learning, failure, frustration and utter rage.

The wonder of this is, as I make these final amendments and additions to the book, I'm writing this as I complete my last week of my notice – doing what I teach and walking the talk.

This has only been possible with the clarity I've gained through my experiences and newer insights coming to the forefront. Even with an excess of 20 plus years of Leadership roles, and 25 years of self-development and goal setting the results have always been mixed.

Up until now, those result have varied from epic minuses to 'off the chart' phenomenal successes, with no rhyme or reason. The confused results ending up with everything thrown in the bin for another year only to try it out in another format with a slight twist or tweak.

Round and round, it went.

Then the cogs clicked, something made sense and all the concepts and ideas came together in harmony, things began to change radically. When these thoughts became clear for myself in my testing and actioning, it also gained deeper understanding from the way that I was sharing them with others, I then brought them together and designed the 'Purpose Goals Legacy' framework, created the 16-week Mentoring program and brought this; the first of 3 books together to share these ideas and help start you on a new road.

Yes, there will always be other concepts and knowledge to add, I'm not saying this is the only way. These are some of the ways that I've learned up until now. Lessons I am getting results with and am expanding on continually.

25 years of successes, failures and vital lessons are wrapped up in these books, so you can start uplifting and continually improving your results or even the results of your teams and those in your care. A big part of this journey has been about learning my purpose. A core element to learning one's purpose is 'Challenge' a certain level of friction to create movement. When I found these ideas, they challenged me – on a deeper level, they challenged me to be more incredible than yesterday, and this is what and why I bring it to you now.

To challenge your thinking so you can take control of key elements of your life, expand the greatest version of who you are and become more incredible than yesterday.

Simple as that (he says).

You will see from the content and journey I share, how this understanding has impacted my life and how it can impact yours. If you think for one minute this is just contrived from text and video content then you'd be mistaken.

The research has definitely boosted my thinking.

Everything I learned in the real world, on the job, through my successes, my pain and deep reflections of the life I have lived.

My hope in this is you learn to quieten the voice of the critic and start listening to the voice of the champion instead. That's where incredible is.

This book is broken into 3-core elements -

Definitions -

Important terms and how they affect you.

Exercises -

There are lots of questions for you to reflect on and answer. There are also spaces for you to write your answers down right here in the book for easy, personal reference.

Actions -

New skills and habits to implement them, that will help you build momentum and get you where you're designed to be by understanding where you're meant to be.

In order to get the most from each of these 3 aspects, firstly we need to learn a little more about how we learn, not just what we'll learn.

"EXPERIENCE: THAT MOST BRUTAL OF TEACHERS. BUT YOU LEARN, MY GOD DO YOU LEARN."

CS LEWIS -

LEARNING

Here's a variation of something I learned from Jim Kwik about learning –

Your learning, up until now, has been a combination of the experiences and places you've been. To forget these now would be impossible they are the culmination of your growth, the stepping stones and building blocks to your understanding. There are gems in here that need to be treasured accordingly and previous doctrines that need to be revisiting and adjusted.

Through this book we're going to call those elements up and for good reason. Hold on to them.

This acronym to help you focus your thinking and attention is called **PAST**. Park, Active, State and Teach – using this tool it helps us to use our Past to propel our future.

P – Park.

What you already know. Put what you've learned on Pause, just for a moment. You cannot un-see what has been seen, or unhear what has been heard - put it to one side while you assimilate this new data.

The ideas that you learn here will then layer over the top of those old ideas, acting like an architectural blue print or a new design schematic, creating a new depth of structure indicating the possible changes that will occur as you develop and apply them.

In some cases, you'll see where the walls need to come down or a new window is required and in other places, you'll see how the original design is absolutely perfect in its current placing – you may not have noticed before and this book will bring that to life for you.

Part of this process will be helping you to connect the dots going backwards, so never forget what you've learned or experienced – those lessons and experiences are important, they got you here and need to be celebrated.

They are the foundations for the next part of the journey!

"IT'S THE ACTION, NOT THE FRUIT OF THE ACTION, THAT'S IMPORTANT."

MAHATMA GANDHI -

A – Active.

Get physically involved with the exercises. Use the work sheets throughout to write down your ideas and responses. The correlation between seeing, reading and writing to boost your learning is huge as you make use of different parts of your brain.

The brain is already using around 30% of its capacity in taking in visual details, bringing physical action into the mix increases the brain dynamic and helps to activate different elements of thinking activity, with writing lighting up the finer motor skill related regions of your head space. Later reading back and seeing things in your own hand writing helps to encode it further and helps you to own it more fully as a personal account.

Read things out loud, activate the sound of your own voice connecting with your ears. Incorporate as many of your senses as you can to stimulate focus and thought around the ideas in this book and the exercises it will ask you to partake in.

When your senses are all engaged the learnings changes shape dramatically.

S - State.

Learning is State dependent. Your level of learning will be impacted by the level of emotion you're working at.

In this book I'm going to ask you to touch upon some of your history for some key events, objectively. This isn't about unpacking traumatic events, this is about cleaning up the building blocks for your future plans and goals by decluttering your launch pad.

It's about enlisting your current self and the parts that lead to here in order to pave a road to a future self that is simply more incredible than yesterday.

This learning is all about connecting to that mind set, that future vision, that emotional space of phenomenal results and growth.
When the emotions dip or drop away your learning will not be at its best – you have to re-engaged with that vision, bring it back to the fore front of your mind to stimulate the thinking.

Action –

Stop where you're at, stand up (back to A.ctive), get a picture in your mind of you 5-years from now more developed, more successful, more grounded and with absolute clarity. Now get that really clear in your head.

How does that feel when you're in that space?

Get those feelings as clear as you can and stand as if you've already achieved everything, you'd ever set out to achieve and with all that clarity refocus and re-join your reading and personal development.

If you're uncertain how this looks or feels, stand as if you do know, stand how you think a role model of yours stands when they're on stage. Stand like Wolverine or She-hulk in the comic books.

Then put the biggest smile you can find on your face and hold it there for more than 2 minutes. Biggest grin.

As the emotions start to raise, and they will, then come back to the learning. Carry that feeling back into what you're doing.

T - Teach.

Share what you learn. The learning will compound in doing so, as Einstein said "If you cannot explain it to a 6-year old, you do not understand it yourself"

Your learning will multiply as you share it with others. Share the tools and concepts to help build your understanding. If you feel inspired to do so, combine these concepts with past learnings to create newer, even stronger concepts, add your own analogies that can help you and those around you go further.

I learned this through martial arts, the experience of sharing what I took for granted with 30-years on and off experience with people of every shape, size and physical capability makes you think faster about physical abilities you take for granted.

Knowing is one thing, knowing and being able to share it in 6-different ways is something completely different. That is the best possible outcome. Learn, teach and expand.

What has come before has brought you to this exact moment, it's not something to forget or regret. We have to absolutely and definitively learn from our past to propel the future.

INFORMATION RICH

Over the coming pages I'm going to share with you the tools and techniques I've learnt, honed and built upon that will help you move from the work you've been taught to do, to the work you're actually designed to be doing and beyond. Stuff that has depth and clarity and is brimming with pride.

For those that want a financial marker on this; I have personally used these concepts to increase my hourly rate by almost 15 times, worked as a consultant and contractor at 4 times my daily salaried role and also secured part times jobs which paid me more than my full time job as I type this.

As a result of me sharing them with my clients and colleagues, I have celebrated them getting multiple promotions, increasing their incomes from 40% up to by 100%. Shortening their working weeks and creating more time and space to spend on personal projects and improving the relationships they have with significant others.

High quality time with high quality people.

For those seeking the emotional, or spiritual aspects of meaning and purpose not necessarily the career adjustments, you will know you are on the right path when you get the feeling of electricity running up your arms and across your face.

You can have both – the electricity and the fair financial trade for what you create with and for others. They do not have to be mutually exclusive.

HIGH QUALITY TIME WITH HIGH QUALITY PEOPLE.

As I said earlier, I want you to park your thinking not forget it.

Here's 3 suggestions of how to use this content –

1. Examine your previous ideas.

Some of your old thinking may serve you, some may not.

2. Over lay new ideas on top.

Be willing to embrace new empowering elements that were previously
absent in your thinking.

3. Infuse new ideas.

Add them with the best of your past thinking to maximise the potential future thinking and outcomes

"A MAN'S MIND IS STRETCHED BY A NEW IDEA OR SENSATION, AND NEVER SHRINKS BACK TO ITS FORMER DIMENSIONS."

OLIVER WENDELL HOLMES SR. -

"A MAN CAN ONLY RISE, CONQUER, AND ACHIEVE BY LIFTING UP HIS THOUGHTS."

- JAMES ALLEN

WHAT IS PURPOSE, GOALS, LEGACY?

When people see or say these words, they tend to be separate. One book talking about goals, a speaker professing about legacy and an ancient wisdom nudging towards our purpose. What I've come to learn is that in order to be fulfilled, we must have all 3 of these elements in play in order to create the incredible – one without the other leads to detrimental behaviours and emotions.

It unbalances the whole.

Although this is the first book of 3 and solely focused on 'Purpose', you need to understand the unrest that comes when we do not have the required, 3-way equilibrium.

Purpose - without Goals and Legacy leads to frustration.

Goals - without Purpose or Legacy often leads to anxiety due to untapped potential.

Legacy - without a clear Purpose or Goal, leads to toxicity and short-sighted destructivity.

It is vital that we have each element included and in balance. We see these three elements in harmony time and time again throughout history with the most beloved individuals and successful characters.

What happens when the balance isn't there?

PURPOSE WITHOUT GOALS AND LEGACY LEADS TO FRUSTRATION

PURPOSE - WITHOUT GOALS AND LEGACY

Purpose without Goals and Legacy is like a blocked pipe. The energy, unable to direct itself, unable to express itself, builds up. Much like the pipe, the weaknesses in the joints become exposed and the welds begin to crack. The pent-up potential backing up, creating immense pressure, and the cracks begin to show as the pipes begin to distort and rupture.

Energy does not dissipate, it redirects. Energy will always find a way.

When we work from a place of undirected Purpose, frustration can bubble up and erupt into anger with catastrophic results - explosive or implosive depending on the tendencies of the beholder. Having a Purpose and not being able to express it positively for the greater good is more damaging than not knowing that you truly have one.

Before Nelson Mandela had clarity on his Goals and what his Legacy would be, he took a different direction, co-founding 'uMkhonto we Sizwe' abbreviated as MK, meaning "Spear of the Nation" the armed wing of the African National Congress (ANC). He sought revenge for previous atrocities, with an understanding of what he wanted to deliver, but not in a way that was of benefit for everyone concerned.

As a result, Nelson was imprisoned for 27 years. In this time though he reconciled his thoughts and he said in relation to his walk to freedom -

"As I walked out the door toward the gate that would lead to my freedom, I knew if I didn't leave my bitterness and hatred behind, I'd still be in prison."

Whilst under harsh conditions, he worked out his goal and he designed a legacy, one that included everyone.

He redirected his energy and created something bigger than himself. People remember more fondly the man that he became once he determined his goals and legacy rather than the anger he manifested before. As a result, he will never be forgotten.

PURPOSE IS THE FOUNDING THOUGHT OF FULFILMENT.

Life growing up for me was fairly straight forward in many ways. I had a stable home life, both parents, both employed and steady schooling.

I was probably considered the creative one, the more intellectually orientated of my brother and I. He was more practical and mechanically hands on, I was more watercolours and kung-fu.

Even from a young age I felt like there was something I was 'meant' to be doing, no idea what, just an early idea, maybe that my name would be up in lights, maybe a far-off childhood ambition.

I would often play towards the centre of attention, whether dancing or entertaining in whatever group I was in. Yet often socially awkward and fairly ok with my awkwardness. I found myself flitting between different social groups and at the same time never quite fitting in.

My parents, both only children, having grown up in very Victorian style settings were now challenged with 2 sons. Where children are seen and not heard, things were very boisterous to say the least. My parents, as yours, did their best with the best they had, for us both.

They were hard working and keen for those ethics to be passed on so we could get a secure job and be comfortable.

This model works for millions. It didn't work for me, and as much as I tried to squeeze myself into it, it never really felt right or worked out. I just felt squeezed and constricted.

I felt like I was doing work I had been 'Told' to do, and I struggled. I had a purpose, but couldn't put my finger on it. Later on in life I realised that I felt I was being forced to work for a salary on someone else's agenda.

I was under achieving and had no other means to escape or evolve. I'd shied away from university, fearing the debt that went with it, botched my school exams as I finished up secondary school and was convinced there was no way out or up.

I was stuck being told what to do and when to do it.

I took my first ecstasy tablet at 16 years old and had been smoking marijuana for a year already. I was self-medicating early on. I didn't learn or realise this until much, much later. The self-medicating anesthetising escalated over a number of years, peaking at 24, with a climatic quantity of drugs that no one in their right minds aspires to.

I knew I had a purpose and felt like I had no way to express it, I began to fold in myself. Numbing out the ambition and the thinking that might have push me forward.

We all have a Purpose, and we *all* need to understand how to connect to it in our daily lives and in what we bring to the world.

Why? Because it's in our nature to do so and failure to do so is harmful.

ALL 3 MUST BE INCLUDED

Purpose, Goals, Legacy is a 3-way, tri-union to create a fulfilled life.

Regardless of our environment, regardless of the perceived adversity, when we have these in place, we can achieve anything. Even in the most horrendous places, at the edges of the darkest points of humanity. When we employ this union, anything and everything is possible.

Whilst speaking of the need for Purpose and doing purposeful work I was challenged by an audience member that not everyone has a choice, I countered with the story I know of Viktor Frankl.

His sense of clarity in this space is a great example of someone with the drive and tenacity to bring each element to life.

A neuroscientist driven by the cause of understanding the human condition. Even faced with a concentration camp through World War 2 he was still completely on purpose and absolutely deliberate in his actions.

Unfaltering, if not accentuated, by his environment. The unimaginable experience was used as an observation of the human condition under its most extreme demonstration of deprivation in its darkest form.

His purpose was to comprehend and share his understanding of the human mind. This Purpose fuelled Frankl, even in a concentration camp. Even in the most insidious of environments entrenched in utter hell.

Yet he watched, learned and even documented. He would find pieces of paper to document his thinking, note his realisations.

When the Nazi's found, confiscated, or destroyed the papers, he would start again. He was driven by his intrinsic values and inspired to share his insights so others could learn from this dimension of the human psyche.

He had a clarity of purpose so strong that he started to craft ways to bring it to life. He had a goal that he clung to throughout his experience. He had the desire and intention of helping the generations yet-to-come avoid the horrors of this first-hand experience he'd come to know.

Now his book, 'Man's Search for Meaning' has been translated into 24 languages and sold over 10 million copies. All because he had each element in play with unmoveable clarity - not for himself, for others to learn from. To be able to help compel others to never return to this diabolism again.

"EVERYTHING CAN BE TAKEN FROM A MAN BUT ONE THING:

THE LAST OF THE HUMAN FREEDOMS - TO CHOOSE ONE'S ATTITUDE IN ANY GIVEN SET OF CIRCUMSTANCES, TO CHOOSE ONE'S OWN WAY."

- VIKTOR FRANKL

WE CAN LEARN FROM THIS

We must stabilise what it is we bring to each of these 3 parts.

For me and my specialisation in coaching, I have supported this balance especially in what people do for their work and also how they connect with their work.

In the vast majority, we spend more time travelling to and from and at work then we do any other activity in our 7-day weeks. Some say, around 60% of our life is at 'work'. We often wear the job title as a label of who we are in relation to the work. John the plumber, Bob the Vicar, Jane who works at the call centre.

As individuals we absorb what we do for so many hours and identify ourselves completely as that thing. In some case's people have trouble removing themselves from the role for fear of losing their identity.

When we think about how important each of these 3 elements are, and when we apply this emotional logic around our job, we can see why we attach, label and cling to the work we do so dearly.

It is perceived as our only way to express these 3 things.

We have a *Purpose* – we have customers to serve, teams to lead, mouths to feed.

We have *Goals* – given to us in line with company objectives

We have a *Legacy* – the organisation continues on doing what it's doing even after you leave.

But.... None of it is yours.

It's someone else's.

What about you?

What about what you want to create in the world, and now as space travel starts to expand how about in the universe?

What's your version of incredible? What does fulfilment look like according to you?

"IF YOU HAVE A STRONG PURPOSE IN LIFE, YOU DON'T HAVE TO BE PUSHED.

YOUR PASSION WILL DRIVE YOU THERE." - ROY T. BENNETT

THE 4 STAGES OF WORK

People rarely understand how truly phenomenal they are. Because they've never been taught how to deliberately design their challenges in front of themselves in order to create that version of incredible.

What does an incredible future look like to you?

Is it the kind that energises you to jump out of bed and go and doing meaningful or purposeful work? Or is there a blocker, a frustration?

In this section I'm going to break down the 4 stages of work so you can see where you are and how you can start moving to the next level and start cultivating that feeling that does energise you to jump out of bed every morning.

You have to know where you are before you can start moving forward. Like SatNav. A SatNav requires 2 pieces of information, 2 points of reference. The first where you are right now, the second where you see yourself arriving, the destination.
What is your relationship to the work you do and create? Where are you right now?

Find that and you can start to move forward, to whatever the destination or the next level looks like to you.

As Peter Sage taught me (and I will definitely repeat later in these books)

"You can't buy a ticket to anywhere but here"

What station are you at and where do you want to get to?

THE 4 STAGES -

- **Taught** – The work we learn to do from the school system.
- **Told** – The work we feel we're being told to do.
- **Meaningful** – Work that is full of meaning to you.
- **Purposeful** – Work that is full of meaning to you, and full of purpose to someone else.

Each stage is an evolution of thinking through your life and your career. Each stage has pro's and con's.

Each stage has some core symptoms that demonstrate where you are. You may be conscious or unconscious of them but in order to progress through them, in the majority, they must be made conscious.

The progressive step has to be made consciously in order to create the desired outcome - as Marshall Goldsmith's book title states, 'What got you here, will not get you there' the haphazard approach works for seldom few.

As you become more aware and you start to have a desire to transcend, and actually start to shift your thinking, the progressive steps cause the cons of the earlier stages start to outweigh the pro's. In this the pressure will start to mount, it will force a movement of some sort; an intolerance or pain point.
How you direct that movement and where you focus that energy will dictate where you move to or stay put.

And let me state for the record at this point in the book, I am not encouraging you to suddenly resign from your post
or be a terrorist inside your organisation. It is about encouraging you to do greater work where you are, thus creating a space to evolve from it, harmoniously.

Whether that be internally or the awakening of a new possibility externally.

It's about naturally becoming too big for the role and evolving beyond it.

On the following pages we'll see what the 4 stages look like and more importantly find out what they feel like, I'll happily share some of my experiences along the way.

"YOU CAN'T WALK UP TO THE TICKET OFFICE OF LIFE AND ASK FOR A TICKET TO ANYWHERE BUT HERE."

PETER SAGE -

STAGE 1 - THE WORK WE'RE TAUGHT TO DO

This isn't a window to bash the schooling system; this is a highlight of the current model (not judging, just reporting).

It isn't working.

With that in mind, some places are already evolving beyond this current concept of education, a different model of learning is being adopted by some families and organisations. Schooling, as a whole, is shifting. What I'm sharing here is my understanding of the impact that it's had and is still having on newer generations in its current format.

What we have, has pros and cons. What I do know is that as people we have an ability to think in different ways which can shape humanity vastly, if not completely. Yet the system isn't prepared or equipped to hold that space. Our here and now the school system of 2019 has not changed in over 100 years and has not yet caught up to us and our newer approach to thinking.

It is a model designed and deployed post-industrial revolution. A factory model to create factory workers. With a view to mass produce workers to supply the factories with a work force at various levels of industry. It's an easily replicable framework that provides a level of consistent output of intellect to man the posts of various levels of industry.

"FOR MOST OF US THE PROBLEM ISN'T THAT WE AIM TOO HIGH AND FAIL - IT'S JUST THE OPPOSITE - WE AIM TOO LOW AND SUCCEED." - SIR KEN ROBINSON

Regardless of the level you are educated to, or the level of qualification you exit with, you are being prepared to step into a hierarchical framework. In most cases you have been graded and supported by your teachers in order to fill a specific quota of individuals at a specific pass rate inside that model. It is a preparatory mechanism to leave the educational institution and go to work.

You attend on X number of days between hours A and B with a set number of days away to rest and wind down (this latter part only being introduced much later on in the working history). The newer concept of schooling; 'Academies' now match the more flexible hours we keep for work. With more mature years now attending a varied spectrum of start and stop times, working in varying sized teams and classes, again as a reflection of the professional outside world. School has changed to match and support it rather than develop it.

With this understanding, it is easy to see that, regardless of the lessons we look to attend, what school we were a part of or the level we attained school is only really teaching us 3 things –

1. Turn up on time.
2. Do as we're told.
3. Live up to someone else's expectation.

It creates a level of uniformity and conformity with which we can measure and monitor for both efficiency and effectivity of the group and the individual.

It gives us predictable behavioural outcomes in certain situations. With this in mind, we can then extend this standardisation and measurement across the globe and into the future. Giving us a reasonably reliable view point of the economic stability as a result of the educational grading systems.

In this model we learn by rote and it creates certainty, that 'uniformity' gives us a base line of capability; Reading, Writing, Arithmetic.

In contrast this damages the ability to be flexible and creative in times of uncertainty. Without the preparation to be innovative personally or professionally it doesn't encourage differences in thought, debate, out of the box thinking or solutions when given curve balls.

How does this impact on our professional lives?

We strive for that conformity. We strive to fit in and not step out of line. We work hard to please our bosses, managers and if we're truly lucky maybe an actual leader.

We make sure we tick every box to meet an exacting standard. We check in and are checked upon, if we're very lucky, once a month or less lucky twice a year. Sometimes, not at all.

We make sure we have someone else's objectives and we work toward helping someone else crest the top of their mountain – mostly without the clarity of whether this is even a mountain we wanted to climb, as in was it truly us that decided it rather than a learned behaviour or someone else's expectation.

SYMPTOMS

- **Security -**

You know where to go and what to do in order to get paid. A structured framework of expectations to work within. A fixed job description of what and when. Simple as that, and the bigger the organisation the bigger the feeling this creates for you.

It keeps you safe and helps people to see what you're doing as safe. Minimising the so-called threat instincts inside the primordial brain and everyone is happy.

- **Fitting in and not standing out -**

Doing what everyone else around you is doing reduces the threat level and eliminates the discomfort through the collective camouflage.

As a result, though individualism is impacted and free thinking is impinged upon, it's making sure we don't challenge the status quo and don't rock the boat. In some cases, this may also be displayed most prolifically as "That's not my job" as people feel uncomfortable going above and beyond, or stepping outside their known remit.

- **Anxiety -**

"Am I doing enough?"
"Am I living up to the expectation?"
"Am I meeting the grade?"

Rather than being encouraged to run your own race and develop your own strengths, you are instructed to live up to someone else's subjective expectations and measuring stick.

It is changing. The school model is shifting and flexing, slowly.

More and more people are starting to understand how the system is working them and their children. As more people are starting to question the frame work and as a result of this questioning, we are seeing higher numbers now home schooling and/or home educating, also a fresh surge of forest and beach schools to support childhood development in natural environments.

I struggled with school as soon as I hit 10 years old.

As I said earlier, my energy was massively depleted by hearing a repetition. I just stopped being interesting, the subjects being put upon me seemed pointless and un-referenceable.

My Parents loved me very much (they still do), I am extremely blessed in this, and they wanted nothing but the best possible outcomes with what we had available as a family and individually.

They both grew up in austere times. My Father's Mother didn't have an indoor toilet until the mid-90's, extremely unheard of here in the UK. They both became police officers which is how they met.

Like every healthy minded parent, they wanted their children to have more than them, to supersede their lot in life.

"THE QUEST FOR CERTAINTY BLOCKS THE SEARCH FOR MEANING. UNCERTAINTY IS THE VERY CONDITION TO IMPEL MAN TO UNFOLD HIS POWERS." — ERICH FROMM

In order to encourage me to succeed beyond them the key questions he'd often asked me early on in my academic life, as well as early professional career –

"What are you going to be?"

"What are you going to do?"

My father wanted me to secure a managerial role, excel and get qualifications to make this happen. An idea of a concrete, stable structures behind me to avoid going through any of the hardships that they had seen or experienced in his early years.

In one sense he was helping me, in another it was creating a tension, a frustration which I didn't know how to positively direct.

I was later introduced the term 'Gen Xen' the in-between of hard-working Gen X and those tipping over into Millennials, in part this helped explain some of my frustrations.

I and the school system simply didn't mesh or gel, I knew early on I had something else to give and at the same time there was no real focal point to bring my attention to or pull me forward.

Eventually I moved into a lower management job (with the help of my Father) and started ticking the boxes. The job had more of a challenge, it kept my interested. I filled in my 1-2-1's, I worked on someone else's objectives, even had them written on my plan by someone else for the year.

I worked hard, I'd get promoted, I'd move somewhere else to get a pay rise. Constantly moving and attempting to find the next best foot hold.

Because that's what everyone does. Chase the promotion, meet an expectation, line up a new job, create security – the one thing my father wanted more than ever for me. He'd grown up through hard recessions, 18% mortgages and large-scale union strikes, mass power black outs.

He wanted stability for me.

Work hard, make the grade and retire.

It never, ever felt right for me – I felt like I was the odd one out. I didn't want to work like this, struggling with what I thought I was capable of, struggling to get enough to do something exciting.

I'd dropped out of school – I'd let myself be labelled a drop out. No real substantial qualifications, petrified by the debt of university so made the assumption I'd amount to not very much based purely on what I thought I didn't have and what I thought others thought of me.

Work hard, work for someone else smarter or luckier than you, and it'll be ok.

It's working for everyone else, so what's wrong with me?

My father's words were encouraging, in actual fact he was goading me in some sense. In part tensioning me, like a spring, because he didn't know any better. Those 2 questions were the full extent of his questioning skills.

Inversely, it really was the start of the journey to now.

There and then, what that frustration achieved was to move me at a very early age, around 15 or 16 years old, to the second stage of work – 'The work that we're Told to do'

"CONFORMITY IS THE JAILER OF FREEDOM AND THE ENEMY OF GROWTH"

JOHN F KENNEDY -

STAGE 2 – WORK WE'RE TOLD TO DO

This happens at the moment you start to realise, or get a feeling that there is more to work and life, than this. There is something that you are 'meant' to be doing or giving, yet don't know what, how or why.

You simply know there's more than what you're doing right now, potentially uncertain where to find the answers, or even the questions to ask.

You're starting to question the work you're doing. Trying to find out the significance to it, you realise how the model works and you begin to comprehend that this frame work does not fit who, or how, you are. More importantly you ask what do I have to offer and what you could I potentially bring?

At this stage you may not realise what your fullest potential is, but you do know you're not able to bring it in the current format.

Who likes being told what to do? Honestly, nobody. In the majority, and depending on the job role, no one likes to be 'told' what to do.

Some careers intrinsically demand that you must be ordered to think in a certain way so that when push comes to shove, we rely fully on the training we've received. The Military is one such job choice.

In other types of employment, those roles lacking the ability or potential to push our thinking, those appearing to be monotonise or lacking any new avenues of growth can give us a level of resentment.

When working with this background resentment it can become very apparent in how we deliver and complete that work. As human beings we need novelty and we need new ways to express ourselves mentally, physically and emotionally.

Otherwise we feel repressed, frustrated and imprisoned.

SYMPTOMS

- **Structure -**

You know exactly where you stand in the hierarchy. You get told one thing so you can tell someone else. Whether this be someone in your managerial line or the customer on the phone. As a result of the high levels of certainty and security this hierarchy creates, we start to feel and miss our own missed potential.

As we start to push at the edges of this, we get told to behave and stay in line. New ideas are either stolen, ignored or ridiculed.

- **Frustration -**

You can't see what other people see, and they can't see what you see. Sometimes it feels like you're talking to a brick wall or you're speaking a different language.

"Am I meeting the grade, or being graded like meat?"

- **Anger -**

The frustration boils over because people just don't get it. Relationships start to tense up, you feel held back in your job and you start to question everything. You attempt to question the framework, normally done emotively and if verbalised causing upset from your peers. Labelled anarchic in some way shape or form, a potential boat rocker.

- **Depression -**

You don't feel like you're living at your full potential, stifled, frustrated and confined. Unchallenged and unfulfilled. You know there's more, but don't know where to go to move forward. The energy you have gets directed elsewhere, more often to numbing mechanisms.

This depression is quiet.

Unseen, accepted and very tolerated.

In Johan Hari's retelling of his horrendous ordeal of being poisoned after eating an apple drench in pesticides in Vietnam he explained that whilst demanding medication to stop the nausea the doctor declined his request. The words he relayed through the translator;

"You need your sickness so we know what is wrong with you"

Meaning, he was using the physical symptoms as the indicator to find out what is wrong with the patient.

The challenge with the symptoms of hating your job, the heart break that comes with the mechanised, factory style clocking in and clocking out for some people you rarely, if at all, see it.

It is so common and pervasive that it's considered normal.

The result is you're never able to pin point the root cause. Maybe, just maybe it's time to look at the place where you spend most of your time, with a bunch of people that feel the same. Because it's slowly degrading you.

We take our 40 hours of frustration a week, plan for the weekend and complain about it to our family, friends and all - over social media and then still go back on Monday morning at 9am because we think someone else thinks we should.

Compounded by this fact from Menshealth.com research –

"the risk of heart attack was 11 percent higher on Mondays than control days, which the researchers defined as Tuesdays through Fridays. Young, working people seemed most vulnerable to the Monday increase—their risk of heart attack was 20 percent higher on the first day of the workweek"

Why? Because they got so fu**ing sick of it a major health incident had to give them a reality check.

"IF THE FREEDOM OF SPEECH IS TAKEN AWAY THEN DUMB AND SILENT WE MAY BE LED, LIKE SHEEP TO THE SLAUGHTER."

GEORGE WASHINGTON -

https://www.menshealth.com/health/a19524979/heart-attack-timing

It takes time to get to this space though. It's a steady drip of stress hormones built up with the constant quiet unhappiness. No light at the end of the tunnel other than retirement which you
get to enjoy when you're no longer physically able to do what you'd like to do with your spare time at that time.

A heart attack is not the (best) answer to get off the hamster wheel and get time off – honestly!

My challenges started at school, 1989, started secondary school or high school as it seems to be Americanising to. I struggled
there. It just didn't fit me or I it. Some would say these were the normal throws of adolescence, of every day schooling. For me it simply didn't feel right, I felt constrained, I felt forced to play small, to not step out of line or the norm. It was suffocating whilst wanting to be different and express myself. I railed against the system and fought anyone and anything I could get my teeth into.

With the bullying I mentioned previously, I steadily hid the vulnerable part of myself away. I didn't know what to do with the hurt, so I stoppered my own personality and directed my pain onto other people. The bullied became the bully, the prey the predator - not knowing what to do I gave the pain to other people in an attempt to make me feel better.

I later learned that *"hurt people, hurt people"*

In truth, it doesn't work like that. You squash yourself down, and close the hurt part away so you can keep it safe. You use
violence and malice to redirect other people's attention away from the parts you don't want to expose. The vulnerable bits closed behind strong doors where no one else can go. I didn't know what to do with it, didn't know how to open that up.

Or even want to.

The frustration of this physical and emotional suffering combined with the stifling of my own self, turned to self-medication.

The bullying of others was part of this. Not an excuse, a reality, I didn't know any better. Smoking, drinking, cannabis, ecstasy. I felt like a deflating balloon, shrivelled and limp yet when you squeezed it the wrinkled latex squeezes out of the available gaps, distorting in different directions wanting to escape and unable to.

Yet when you let go, its deformed shape still remains a little. And by the way; no drug is a gate way to another drug – traumatized, unsupported thinking is the gate way to the misuse of drugs. A lack of connection and community post any sort of abuse is the gateway to addiction.

I had a pent-up energy, a creative force to be expressed, yet didn't know how to without being or feeling hurt somehow.

The weakness had to stay in the past.

I didn't know the right questions to ask, didn't have people around me to ask the deeper questions I ask others now. It felt like I was rotting from the inside out. That's why the protective habits started to form. A lack of focus and direction started to shift my thinking and without realising, I ended up in a very dark place. As I have mentioned and will mention again later – it almost cost me my life.

I stayed here too long. I got lost, didn't know where to turn and the hurt just got too much. The deeper reality; the hurt person was hurting the same person – me.

Large numbers, huge percentages, of people do exactly I as did. They simply stay in these first 2 stages of work. Unhappy, unengaged and going through the motions. Either, happily oblivious to what is possible or consciously ignoring their full potential until it becomes a habit.

Whether conscious or not if we do start to comprehend or get a feeling for what we can do and don't know what to do with it, the anger and depression starts. With a feeling of being confined, constricted and cuffed to the system.

I began to implode, deteriorating from the inside out, quite literally.

In this space it is very easy to get stuck, the 'Law of Conformity' kicks in – in short, an idea where if everyone else is doing it, and appears to be right, that you'll start or continuing doing it also.

If you hang out with 10 drug dealers and addicts, you'll become the 11th.

Likewise, if you hang out with 10 millionaires it's pretty certain that you'll start to infuse that knowledge and understanding and will become the next one in the group to hit 7 figures (a preface to habits in books 2 and 3 – hang out with great people; virtually and physically)

How this works for us is firstly, we look around and check if everyone else is having any issues. We either gauge they're not and then consider that it must just be us and rather than speaking out we keep quiet in order to maintain the order.

Not challenging the status quo and in doing so not having to initiate the dialogue we've been avoiding with ourselves for so long. To avoid the deeper work, the 'Hard work' we start to build our tolerance to our surroundings. We bottle it up. In fact, we bottle ourselves up even further.

And then, secondly, we 'flock'. Congregate with our colleagues and take part in group bitching and moaning around the water cooler or printer with zero impact on what is actually happening.

In this we return to building up a tolerance to the circumstance by sympathising with our team mates. We gather together to feel better.

Either way, the side effect of this is a constant stream of cortisol; stress hormones.

The steady drip of tension and a steadily increasing brain chemical over load resulting in physical and mental toxicity and ill health.

Let me repeat that this is something we have been learning for a long, long time; fitting in, conforming and staying in line.
More importantly, someone else's line.

Because if we do step out of it, we'll be challenged back to fit the requested requirements. So, we do. We fit in, in order to 'stay safe' and in order to counter act this as human beings, on the whole, take action to equalise or negate the stress by so called relief techniques.

What we actually see as the core symptoms of those stuck in this mind set is; self-medication.

For example; high risk and/or inappropriate sexual activity, drugs (legal/illegal socially acceptable or not), gambling or gaming.

Compulsive, unhealthy activities individually from this list or a combination of all of them depending on how far we go.

Even over working, too much coffee and excessive use of social media. These are all dopamine focused activities to give the brain something else to think about other than the current 'tolerated' circumstance.

They are all Distractions. Warning signs.

If we find ourselves doing things that are either ways out of or avoidance tactics from work, then we have some fairly clear indications we're doing the wrong things with our time.

Are you looking for an excuse not to focus on what you're being paid to do? Or hiding behind the activities of those around you to avoid discussing it?

If you're not fully focused on what you're doing or fully engaged then these are already the symptoms you may be in the wrong job/career, company or industry. Life is designed to be interesting, there are numerous memes proliferating about leading lives where you don't need a vacation, doing jobs that don't feel like work. They are absolutely possible. Opportunities and careers like this exist.

The 2016 Gallup Poll showed the British economy lost just under £84 Billion in lost productivity due to a lack of engagement from the national work force. This number doesn't even factor in potential sickness/absence through the year.

This lost productivity is as a result of huge swathes of people not being engaged in their work, let alone their work even attempting to engage them – it's a 2-way street. Does what we do stimulate us or us it?

We need to be doing work we actually want to do, that we are designed to do and in no way feel obligated to do.

How do we know we're in the wrong job role or career?

£84 BILLION IN LOST PRODUCTIVITY?

As a Leader and consultant in some extremely 'Challenging' environments, where people aren't the driving focus of the business here's the common (and ignored) 3 tells, I've personally done, experienced and witnessed from my 20 years of Leadership & Coaching.

1.   'Monday Morning' or 'Post Holiday Blues' and 'Working for the Weekend' -

As the weekend starts to wind down and the pending thought of Monday looms, has waking up at the start of the week become a drag?

Is the getting ready for work a chore and at times worse, even loathsome?

This sensation is a massive indicator that something is definitely amiss.

How many times has your holiday started to come to a close and the dread of work starts to roll up on you like a shadow and all the joy leeches out of the previous 2 weeks? Do you need a holiday straight after the holiday? From the moment you're back at work does it feel like a life time ago or a distant memory? If this is the case then you absolutely need to take time to review what it is you're doing, creating and putting into the world.

These symptoms might appear obvious, however, 100's of thousands of people struggle every day to go to work.

In 2017 85% of the globally employed weren't happy in their work – yet they drag themselves in time and time again to a job they 'tolerate' and/or to a boss they potentially feel obliged to work for.

According to this Gallup poll it breaks down like this - 2 thirds of the people polled were described as *"not engaged"* meaning they are *"unhappy but not drastically so"*.

Gallup's definition of these people is;

"Employees are psychologically unattached to their work and company. Because their engagement needs are not being fully met, they're putting time — but not energy or passion — into their work."

They've checked out. They were punching the right number of buttons to get by, stay under the radar and deliver just enough, no more.

This leads to a huge down turn in productivity 18% are what Gallup calls "actively disengaged" again, Gallup's definition here is;

"Employees aren't just unhappy at work — they are resentful that their needs aren't being met and are acting out their unhappiness. Every day, these workers potentially undermine what their engaged co-workers accomplish"

"They pretty much hate their jobs. They act out and undermine what their co-workers accomplish."

"OH, YOU HATE YOUR JOB? WHY DIDN'T YOU SAY SO? THERE'S A SUPPORT GROUP FOR THAT. IT'S CALLED EVERYBODY, AND THEY MEET AT THE BAR."

- DREW CAREY

As a result, there is an increased amount of time off for physical and mental health, higher attrition culminating in additional recruitment costs due to lost staff – and that isn't exclusive to the individual. This also includes the people they relate to on a daily basis and how they impact on their fellow colleague's mental wellbeing. Emotions are contagious.

15% are engaged - Is this truly possible that they're really holding up the economy?

Bear in mind, this 15% is the global result, in Western Europe this is only 10%.

As a mental health, personal wellbeing and business model, how is this sustainable?

How much did I say was lost in the UK alone due to productivity issues?

Multiple 10's of millions every year.

https://www.gallup.com/workplace/231668/dismal-employee-engagement-sign-global-mismanagement.aspx

https://www.gallup.com/workplace/238079/state-global-workplace-2017.aspx?
utm_source=link_wwwv9&utm_campaign=item_231668&utm_medium=copy

What's the impact?

In absenteeism alone, these is an astronomical amount of money being lost due to this disconnect from our daily activities.

Further surveys and research completed by the Labour Force Survey across 2017/2018 here in the UK showed a staggering number of days off;

15.4 million days off connected to work-related stress, anxiety and depression.

It's a very easy connection between employee disengagement to days off.

When I did the math, on average, minus weekend and holiday days we spend 42% of our total days on this planet, at work.

And honestly there are plenty of people still thinking about their 'jobs' on the weekend.

It's right to assume that what you spend the largest portion of your life doing is going to have a huge impact on the quality of your life.

Gallup backed this assumption up for me; companies where people are engaged in their work experience have a 41% lower absentee rate.

It goes to show these numbers are not mutually exclusive, what we do at work is having a huge impact on our Mental wellbeing.

It is only now, more recently, with high visibility individuals talking about their mental health that this is becoming more widely talked about.

Mental Health in the work place is high on the agenda of every right-thinking leader and organisation, and it's not just affecting young workers or millennials. It concerns everyone young and old, male and female without discriminate on colour or creed.

What we are now beginning to understand is we all have a level of mental health exactly the same as our physically health and we need to look after it The Labour Force Survey (UK only) continued to show that;

In 2017/18 stress, depression or anxiety accounted for 44% of all work-related ill health cases and 57% of all working days lost due to ill health.

They documented for this time period there were 595,000 workers suffering from work related stress, depression or anxiety.

And these are only the cases that get discussed or diagnosed due to stigma, embarrassment and even down to the financial implications of having to advise your life assurance providers. The latter I found out recently when reviewing ours.

Out of those cases that are reported here are the reasons broken down;

- Workload – 44%
- Lack of Support – 14%
- Violence/Bullying – 13%
- Changes at work - 8%
- Other - 21%

www.hse.gov.uk/statistics/causdis/stress.pdf

Health and safety at work Summary statistics for
Great Britain 2018 - http://www.hse.gov.uk/statistics/overall/hssh1718.pdf

From an employer/employee perspective, a job needs to be engaging – the work we do needs to be physically and mentally stimulating as well as emotionally energising.

Physically -

We dedicate most of our days to sitting at a desk punching numbers on a computer. Rather than moving, we spend huge amounts of money of ergonomic furniture to make the sitting more comfortable instead of actually doing something about it. It's important we make space to stretch, move, walk around the building and reconnect with people. Take a 10-minute refresh outside at lunchtime. Very few jobs physically push us. Exercise creates endorphins and once upon a time the physical act of gathering food as a member of the tribe made us feel good, yet we sit at a desk barely moving, sedentary and physically unhappy.

Mentally -

We're learning things to accomplish a job we feel beholden to with little time to learn for ourselves. Benjamin Franklin committed 1 hour a day to learning, on any subject he enjoyed – it stimulates brain activity, promotes neural regeneration and keeps the mind open to new thinking.

Timothy Leary said *"You're only as young as the last time you changed your mind"* Which at the same time would be hugely beneficial to any role you do; new ideas create new possibilities.

A new possibility may even make the job you're doing actually A) interesting, B) potentially easier or C) create something new and of value to the business you work in.

All of which potentially leads to promotion – being visibly bored and unproductive tends to have the opposite effect.

Emotionally -

Does what you're doing align with who you are? Does it enable you to achieve your goals by helping others achieve theirs? Who are you working for and how do you relate to them? If there is no emotional bond you will simply never fully engage.

Why would you? A job has to cover all 3 of these in order to firstly, propel you out of bed every morning and secondly, maintain your full attention all day, every day, not just Friday and especially not just before a 2-week holiday while you're tying up loose ends so you can put your out of office on.

When we have a purpose and are doing purposeful work – no matter the size of challenge, those challenges become exciting.

We find support or make decision more easily and if someone starts to micro-manage us or bully us, we either simply set the right boundaries or go where we can find the trust and security, we know we need and are worthy of. We know we truly deserve it so we don't sit in sufferance.

Work absolutely must be exciting.

"YOU'RE ONLY AS YOUNG AS THE LAST TIME YOU CHANGED YOUR MIND"

TIMOTHY LEARY -

2. Social media and the toilet -

Life is full of distractions. All the time we are bombarded by advertising and messaging everywhere we look. Social media has become a socially acceptable disengagement from the world.

How many times have you sat on the toilet and checked Facebook, Insta or WhatsApp?

How many times have you sat legitimately or even just to escape the office and heard the person next to you quickly kill the volume on the 'Ex-Factor Golden ticket winner' blaring out of their cubicle?

Whilst at work I have personally pushed a toilet door open as it showed vacant, only to find a person sitting on the toilet lid just so they could get time away from their desk. They weren't even using the toilet - thankfully.

According to research by Rebootonline.com, they highlighted that around three hours and five minutes of a working week is spent on social media.

Along with the daily procrastination of over 2 hours this is equating to companies paying out on average £8,851.14 per employee per year on distracted time.

On the other side of this – you're using your mobile phone in the toilet.

In a recent online Times magazine article, they stated

'Your Cell Phone Is 10 Times Dirtier Than a Toilet Seat'

https://time.com/4908654/cell-phone-bacteria/

https://www.rebootonline.com/blog/survey-reveals-how-much-time-we-really-waste-in-the-working-day/

Not surprising then as to why your phone has so much bacteria in it if you use it whilst using a public toilet.

You touch the door, lift the seat, smear your finger round the screen and then put your mouth next to it and inhale.

Take a moment to digest that.

Literally.

When you are focused, deliberate and on purpose sneaking off to the toilet to check your tweets before pulling 2-ply sheets doesn't really come into the thinking.

Fire fighters, don't think they'll nip off for a wee and check out 'I Hate my Job' on Facebook when emergencies are taking place.

Emergency room nurses don't think about travel locations on Instagram or checking their Tinder notifications while they're saving lives.

They are engaged.

Full intention with their attention.

How long you keep yourself distracted is a good indicator of how off kilter things are, and where you keep yourself distracted also has implications on your health.

3. Getting sick or worse still, faking sick -

As a human being you are actually designed to run optimally, based on the right hormones and chemicals being released into your system as a result of your environment, food and the relationships you have personally and professionally. When things aren't in the best possible place, stress hormones either flood or flush the system. You end up with a constant and continuous stream being released over extended and protracted periods of time.

The result; the immune system suffers. It slows down and things just don't work the way they're meant to and we get sick.

Depending on the level of tolerance we have and the length of time we expose ourselves to these scenarios can provide an indicator as to the severity of the illness that results.

This can be challenging to highlight, as normally this has built up over a period of time with the threshold of tolerance steadily increasing as the pressure starts to mount. We often don't see this until something, or someone breaks.

One early warning sign is sickness at the start of a holiday. As soon as the pressure releases the system flushes and allows the brain to process everything that is happening. We have time to rest, recuperate and process our stress physically.

An alternative to this; there are those that have or are planning to fake sickness. This is an easier red flag to see because you're starting to plan time off to compensate for the energy that has been sapped whilst doing a job you don't like.

This is the opportunity to hide away from people we 'have to' associate with.

Unable to leave the house in case of being seen out. There is a potential for further isolation as individuals stay indoors again plugging into social media or gaming to fill the time. The perceptions about the job driving a low feeling that builds to a constant sensation that gradually turns into depression. In one metric I recently read, the current average for days off due to depression is 27 days a year. People are simply lacking purpose or a feeling of meaningful contribution and would rather hide themselves away than do what they're "contractually obligated" to accomplish.

Neither of these spaces are healthy to be in, both impacting on mental health and ultimately on productivity and the growth of any business.

How do you know if you're there? When we live in these states the language that we use is very much around blame and victimhood in all its various guises. The 'To Me' mentality.

"You wouldn't believe what was done to me"

"It's not my fault, it's the type of customer that come through to me"

If this is true in your life, check in with yourself.

Start thinking about what you believe you're designed to be doing. Bring your attention to what would and does engage you, what parts of your job do hold your attention?

In the modern work place there are few that know there is a way beyond this and fewer still that know the way to move out of this.

What are the tell-tale signs of the 'Work we're Told to Do'?

Firstly procrastination. A quiet insidious killer of dreams and aspirations. Regardless of age, religion or sexual orientation procrastination's rooted in fear. It stops us in our tracks, in fact it keeps us in our track, like a stuck record unable to shift its grove into the next verse of a great song.

No one would ever say they procrastinate; no one would ever want to admit it or lose face over it. Instead they bat away the possibility of what they do by making an excuse Secondly, deeply questioning the work you do on a daily basis.

I've got to the office and sat on the toilet at 08:09 and stared at the back of the door and asked myself;

"What difference does it actually make?"

"What if I went home right now, would any one actually care?"

And then I asked myself the worst question to ever ask yourself, or someone else –

"If all of this were to end right now, what difference will I have made?"

When I asked this of myself, I wasn't talking about completing suicide, I was purely talking about the company I worked for closing its doors and mass redundancy. What difference will I have made in this job to humanity or even my local community?

For me I could see the work would still be there tomorrow, someone else would fill the spot and I'd be forgotten in a heartbeat.

That longing to be elsewhere was immense because I knew I could do something more productive with my time and create a bigger impact working in different spheres. That's when the low mood started to kick in, the early warning signs of depression. I'm lucky in that sense, I know what they are and how they feel.

Some don't.

As I wrote the first draft of this book, still working for a large organisation that only cares if I create 'x' number of widgets in 'y' number of hours.

Because of this lack of people centricity, I get those sensations. I do things that enable me to not do my job in socially acceptable ways. Even acknowledging that to myself, let alone in type to you is painful and woeful.

It's an absolute waste of my own potential.

Those distractions get lost in the excuses we tell ourselves.

THE 3 EXCUSES

1. The 'Not Enough' Excuse -

"I'm not [insert label of choice here] enough – rich, tall, small, white, black, skilled, resourced, gifted, talented, intelligent, educated... enough."

Or, the 'Comparison' variation

"I'm not as [insert label here] - talented, resourced, connected, rich... as them."

You are enough. It got you here, the odds were huge just to make it this far and you defied them. Every decision kept you alive, got you paid, got you promoted. Mine got me married, a nice house, travelled the world all the ups and downs to go with it.

Let me repeat; "What got you here will not get you there." You need to be a better business person, a smarter coder, website building, sales man or woman whatever. Your future demands a certain amount of mental, emotional, physical developing and evolving.

When you say you're not good enough, think about what it is in relation to. The version of you may not be drawing in multiple millions in revenue (yet), you're on the path to make it happen.'Yet' is your friend.

I'm not as talented as... 'Yet'
I'm not smarter enough to... 'Yet'

Remind yourself regularly you're on a journey. Because you are. Your beginning is not the same as someone else's middle or end. They're just further along because they started earlier than you, that's all.

2. The 'Obligation' Excuse -

"I can't do that because I've got a family to feed, keep a roof over their heads...."

"It's too much of a risk because..."

I get it. Honestly, I do.

I played the game for 20+ years, secured ok jobs, built a life framed by certainties and securities. Got married, got a mortgage, became a parent.

Right now, knowing what I know, if it had been 10 years ago, maybe I'd jump ship, move in with my parents, risk it all to give this new life my full attention.

But I can't. I have to tread carefully, create a structure, a bridge to transition me from here to there. 'There' being financial freedom, running my own successful business, an entrepreneur and crafting a new world for future leaders.

And that's ok.

I'm not stuck, I just have to be more thoughtful, tactical and strategic in my moves as I unpick a little of what I've built in order to do what I'm designed to do.

"IF YOU ARE LIVING OUT OF A SENSE OF OBLIGATION YOU ARE A SLAVE ."

WAYNE DYER -

3. The 'What if's' Excuse -

"What if I fail, what will people think?"
"What if I succeed, what will people think?"

The common place we regularly see this excuse is; the failure to apply for a new job.

We stop ourselves taking the promotion in another department or company for fear of what someone else might think about us if we do, or don't get the job.

In truth though, people don't actually care unless they truly wish you ill or truly love you, and that's a really, really small number of people. Most people will blink and have forgotten almost instantaneously. There are very few people that deeply care about you or your successes. People are too wholly wrapped up in their own $h!t to give it a second thought. Yet because you got caught up in thinking what are they thinking about me, you hesitate.

We've all done it, and then justified the absolutely life out of it to make sure we're ok with the inaction!

Each of these excuses turns into idle chit-chat, a justification I'd use to validate my inaction backed up by distraction and then capped off with the self-medication, which leads into self-fulfilling stagnation and eventually regret.

But, no one will ever tell you that, because they're too busy doing it themselves.

During the justification of the procrstination, deeply questioning your current circumstance is a really good place to start taking some time to reflect and start reimagining the future.

THE SCIENCE BEHIND TAUGHT & TOLD BEHAVIOURS –

An experiment carried out in 1967 by Gordon R. Stephenson looks at the learned behaviours of primates. A couple of decades later several current authors and trainers used this experiment as an example of how easy and damaging it can be to teach, embed and maintain an idea inside a group or organisation.

Somehow over the course of time the actual experiment has shifted from its reality into the '5 Monkeys experiment', more a modern-day Aesop Fable than a true-life event. For the true version of events search – 'Cultural Acquisition of a Specific Learned Response Among Rhesus Monkeys'

THE 5 MONKEYS EXPERIMENT (A MODERN-DAY PARABLE FOR PERSONAL DEVELOPMENT)

5 monkeys are placed into a lab environment along with the monkeys inside the lab is a set of ladders with a bunch of bananas hung near the top.

The natural reaction for the monkeys is to attempt to climb the ladder and retrieve the bait, yet each time a Monkeys goes up the ladder, the other monkeys get sprayed with water. Eventually, over time, the Monkeys learn the outcome and every time a monkey attempts to ascend the ladder the other monkeys freak out and attack the adventurous or hungry primate. The resulting behaviour is that none of the apes go up the ladder, no matter how tantalising the treat.

The second stage of the experiment is one monkey is replaced with a new monkey.

The initial reaction, the new monkey sees the bananas at the top of the ladder and goes for them and swiftly gets a beating by the other 4. Over an extended period of time all the monkeys get replaced, in the end none of the present monkeys will attempt to climb the steps. Yet none have actually been soaked with water, none of them ever have any understanding of why they should not climb the ladder.

In several synopsis of the experiment it underlines the most damaging statement in business as well as life. When questioning someone as to why they're doing what they're doing the painful response is;

"It's the way we've always done it"

We simply don't question that which is for fearing of rocking the boat, yet when asked no one else actually knows.

"IT'S THE
WAY WE'VE ALWAYS
DONE IT"

WHO'S AGENDA?

A friend that has recently taken part in my 16-week coaching program threw a couple of questions at me about this when I shared this story.

The wonder of coaching and mentoring is this sort of learning experience is always a 2-way dialogue, simply because there are always new ways to see things.

Sarah asked me this;

"Can't all the Monkeys climb at the same time?"

It makes sense. No monkeys get sprayed because they're all on the ladder.

In truth though; it's not about climbing the ladder, it's more about who's ladder is it any way?

We end up with 5 monkeys scrabbling up a tottering ladder, and without being consciously aware – it isn't even our ladder.

The ladder belongs to the person leading the experiment. It was put there for and on someone else's agenda. Whether that someone believes it's in our benefit or not regardless, it's part of the game.

With the bananas as a temptation to cause a disruption and the water cannon to instil the hierarchy and fear of even attempting to go up the ladder in the first place. Reinforcing the continuing behaviour.

Chase the job, seek a promotion, always be striving for the next accomplishment.

"WE CANNOT FIND FULFILMENT ON THE TRACK OF ACHIEVEMENT."

Especially when the odds feel, or are, in most cases stacked against you.

There are only so many promotional spots you can chase or acquire, and the higher up the chain you go, the less spaces there are.

You don't have 300 CEO's of a company and 1 worker.

Go and find your own ladder, enjoy climbing it not just for the bananas.

"Can't the Monkey's attack the water jet?"

Yes.

In the most common sense, this is called civil disobedience or a union strike. This very rarely ends positively for any one or for any extended period of time.

Cost of living always rises, therefore today's improvement become tomorrow's gripes.

The longer-term plan is to get really conscious about what your bananas really look like, feel like and taste like and also where you get your banana's.

If the Monkey stops playing the game and leaves the experiment to find its own rewards the water jet has nothing to spray.

THE TIPPING POINT

This story became a work of fiction over time. The Monkeys never got to breaking point. For most people eventually, through the use of the neo-cortex, our human psyche snaps in one-way shape or other.

The brain will find ways to overcome, counter act or do something new rather than continue in the oppressive state, the end result, a true shift from the work that we're told to do and the potential frustration.

Regrettably the mechanisms that are provided more commonly are there to numb the sensation in order to facilitate you going back to work and remaining quiet.

The hangover
The comedown
The post orgasmic 'Little death'
The long-term antidepressant regime of ever-increasing dosages as the effects wear off with the law of diminishing returns building its resistance*

*NB I'm not saying flush the drugs down the toilet.

Get help, get a counsellor, learn more about what you are doing, what you are capable of and the need for them wears off.

You've spent a lot of your life learning to need them, you're now going to need to spend a part of your life learning to not need them.

And it is possible.

FRUSTRATION TO IMPACTFUL

What we truly want to do is move away from regret and move towards an incredible, impactful future where you positively touch the lives of everyone you come into contact with.

Is it possible to overcome the previously mentioned excuses?

Absolutely!

Truthfully, everyone started with the same level of resources, skills, obligation.

Everyone starts somewhere –
Richard Branson in a phone box selling records
Tony Robbins in a beat-up VW beetle listening to Jim Rohn or
Tom Bilyeu making protein bars.

You have to remind yourselves regularly that you cannot compare your beginnings to their middles or ends. How is that fair or reasonable to you?

We started with exactly the same as everyone else – nothing. Naked and screaming exactly the same as the next person. It's the way we learn to read our stories and interact in the world that make us different.

Regardless of who else is out there doing something you'd like to do – just get started.

Start doing things that are significant to you and more importantly; to others.

3 ELEMENTS

What makes successful and fulfilled people are 3 core elements.
They all have a grasp on –

Purpose – an absolute clarity on who they are when they're at their best

Goals - aligned to that purpose that impact others

Legacy – taking action on a daily basis. Ones that have phenomenal momentum and create an incredible future way beyond themselves.

When we have these 3 things in place it creates the mental capacity to see a new version of the future and fuels your determination to bring it to life.

I know, with my clarity on these 3 steps I have written this, my first book, coached and trained hundreds if not thousands by the time this goes to press for the first time. As you're reading this, I have launched an online coaching program, overcome hospitalisation several times in my life. Become the father I hoped I would be and have risen myself from self-medicating mediocrity to helping others create their version of incredible. I also know the people I've shared these concepts with have made huge changes also. I've seen them get promoted, raise their own salaries, consciously and unconsciously realigning themselves with their destinies.

As you take these ideas in, spot the symptoms, eliminate the excuses and start taking deliberate action to improve things, you will start to move from taught to told and then into 'Meaningful' work.

This is where fulfilment begins – In things that are meaningful and significant.

"TO GIVE LIFE MEANING, ONE MUST HAVE A PURPOSE LARGER THAN SELF"

- WILL DURANT

THE DIFFERENCE BETWEEN MEANINGFUL AND PURPOSEFUL, AND HOW DO WE GET THERE?

First, I need to explain what 'Meaningful' work is and how this progresses into 'Purposeful'. For me there is a difference, a subtlety in language yet a clear distinction for me.

STAGE 3 - MEANINGFUL WORK

The next level to moving through and out of the work we feel we're 'Told' to do is 'Meaningful' work. It is the first steps to finding satisfaction and creating fulfilment in what you do on a daily basis.

It doesn't matter what your job is, how much you say you hate it or dislike it there are always elements you can find in that role or in an organisation that you can call meaningful in your 9-5.

'Meaningful' work is the kind that is full of meaning to you, and when you do it, it brings a smile to your face as it emotionally charges you to do more of it. You may find this in your hobbies and passions or the simple craft of delivering excellence in a specific part of your current job.

These are the things you love to share at the end of the day with your family of friends. It's not the number of widgets you made that makes it interesting, it's what you find significant that counts.

When you do it, you can get lost in it and actively seek it out wherever you can to do more of it, because who in their right mind wouldn't look for reasons to smile in their day?

SYMPTOMS

- **It makes you smile -**

It's work that brings you joy and a sense of pleasure - so you have to smile, it brings a sense of pride in doing it.

- **You share it -**

When you do it, you get an extra bounce in your step, it energises you, you can do it for hours on it, almost forgetting to eat. Letting your tea or coffee go cold, you engross yourself in it.

Because it feels so good you want to tell others about it and sometimes get frustrate because they can't see the sense of fulfilment you get out of it when you're doing it. You also love telling your family about it when you get home. Those prized moments, those interactions that mean something to you being passed positively forward.

- **You look for new ways to build it -**

You start to find ways to improve it, perfect it and do more of it. Whilst being completely wrapped up in your work you'll actively seek and learn and build it.

Digesting huge amounts of content to perfect the craft. Diving into new ideas and possibilities that enable you to organically redefine what it is you're doing.

Pushing the realms of your potential in delivering this new way or concept.

THERE IS A TRAP – BE WARNED

In 2013, my strongest year of performance so far in the corporate space, I worked intimately with an exceptionally driven team and we focused on being number 1 in every aspect; in sales, in revenue, in attendance, in every possible metric we had.

We went home buzzing every night because we delivered. The team was strong and the outputs said so.

We, as a team, also said so – very loudly and very clearly. Although I thought it was meaningful, it was simply about my significance. I made sure everyone knew we were on top and had the leading performance and everyone else was beneath us. 4 people left my team that year – 2 walked out and 2 never showed for work. This only happened because I was relentless in my pursuit of a sense of meaning by telling people what to do. I dressed it up as one thing in truth spent my time telling people which way to go. I made it the work they were 'Told' to do and called it meaningful to me.

We did great work as a team, but there was and is a better way - People need to feel they have meaning in what they do and are sharing meaningfully. I learned this the hard way. Diminishing my peers to make sure I was No.1, More adversely, making sure that everyone knew it. That's actually Demeaning, removing others significance. There's and mine.

This habit feeds the ego, not the soul. It's just you inflicting a version of the work they're 'Told to do'. It is also wise to remember 50%of people leave managers, not jobs. They leave the people they work for, not the work they actually do.

What you're doing might be what you're good at, it might be making you smile as you bring some of the best elements of you but in some cases, it can become self-serving, selfish and demoralising.

Exercise -

In order to start the road to 'Meaningful' Work and creating fulfilment ask yourself these questions –

- What part of your job do you enjoy the most?
- What is it you're actually doing that makes you smile?
- What people are you connecting with that enables this?
- What help do they ask you for when they most need it?
- What pastimes do you do that you lose yourself in?
- What is it about them that raises your energy?

Answering these handful of questions will help to kindle your thinking in ways to start seeking out different roles and responsibilities in your 9-5.

You'll start to see the world a little differently – rather than dreading every part of the job, you'll start to focus on the bits that bring the most satisfaction.

It doesn't mean you can disregard the other, equally important bits that you don't like. That's why you have a contract in place.

Find these answers to start sparking fulfilment in your here and now to create your there and then.

"THIS IS THE TRUE JOY IN LIFE, THE BEING USED FOR A PURPOSE RECOGNIZED BY YOURSELF AS A MIGHTY ONE...

...THE BEING A FORCE OF NATURE"

GEORGE BERNARD SHAW -

PURPOSE -

PURPOSE IS A FEELING YOU CULTIVATE

Purpose is you at your fundamental best, you with the in-authenticities striped away simply being your profoundest and deepest self. It's about being aware of and breaking away from the expectations that others are attempting to label you with.

Acknowledging them for what they are, and comprehending 'who' you really bring on a daily basis.

This is based on the way you see the world not someone else's perception of you, it's not based on what you think someone else thinks of you.

Instead, you decided to be you.

You decided to unpick the stories that have played out time and time again since you were born until now. Because, inside these stories and events is a language that only you speak. It is a dialect of individualism innate to you. Hard coded and hardwired into your DNA, physically bound at conception. A concept. An idea. Because that's how all things start. As a thought.

Purpose is the thing you do every time and as you learn to speak this truth. You can learn to connect the dots going forward because you unravelled the threads going backwards. You start to understand what is full of meaning to you and is full of purpose to someone else. Things become easier because it's you, being you. That is all. Not trying or pretending – just being your best version, right now. Not a second-rate copy or misguided perceived representation, not a regurgitation of an imagined past or future. It's a right now, you firing on all cylinders, pointed in the right direction doing what you are designed to do at your most incredible.

Purpose is that feeling, we've all touched it at some point, maybe momentarily, maybe for a whole event. An electric feeling of goose bumps up the arms, brimming pride and excitement about a coming event we've created or organised.

Purpose is that sensation.

More often than not though, we shy away from it, believing that it was set to a certain scenario or situation, that was only for then, "who am I to think that's something I can aspire to feel always?"

"We fear our highest possibilities. We are generally afraid to become that which we can glimpse in our most perfect moments, under conditions of great courage." Said Abraham Maslow.

Instead of examining that which we've done, we go back to that which we did and wonder why things simply aren't as exciting as they were.

We get a sensation of stagnation.

Rather than shake the feeling, we fall back into old habits rather than chase white rabbits.

"WE FEAR OUR HIGHEST POSSIBILITIES. WE ARE GENERALLY AFRAID TO BECOME THAT WHICH WE CAN GLIMPSE IN OUR MOST PERFECT MOMENTS, UNDER CONDITIONS OF GREAT COURAGE."

- ABRAHAM MASLOW

Maybe it's some misguided story about dismantling the golden goose that stops us from uncovering a golden truth.

The golden truth is found when we do dismantle what happened. When we do investigate further the feeling we had in that moment and through this prying open it grows, exponentially.

It cannot be diminished by its examination, this does not stop when you cut into it, it gets bigger through your familiarisation. Because we find ways to bring it to life more regularly, we keep these fond thoughts at the forefront of our thinking and inflate them imaginatively so we can do it again and again and again.

The first understanding is that - you have a choice to feel this way.

Being on purpose and creating fulfilment is not for the select few or exceptionally gifted. Yet, when you tap into it, people will be drawn to you because they will perceive you as both; exceptional and gifted. As you craft this and continually shape this, others will see something that is rare and extraordinary. Creating more magnetism and draw.

Someone being deliberate, on their own terms, running their own race and being incredible.

It's a rarity.

When you're focused and deliberately on purpose you cannot be anything but incredible.

If you want to increase fulfilment in your life, you have to move from Meaningful to Purposeful.

16-POINTS ON PURPOSE

1. It is the key to your version of incredible.

When this door unlocks the game truly changes. It untethers you from you're perceived past, you can start mapping the route ahead, attracting the right people into your life and manifesting a life worth seeing flash before your eyes at the very end. This isn't spiritual, 'Law of Attraction' woo-woo.

It's about deliberacy and intention

2. It is not determined by your past or present position in life.

A stained past does not mean a stagnant future. By being on purpose you can focus your actions more clearly, you can be more intentional with your approaches, you can even decipher your previous action to help front load future events with more purpose and more intent action. What I do know is lacking clarity of purpose (consciously or subconsciously) leads to poor thinking and poor choices. No one wakes up and thinks today I'll make a really sh**ty mess of my life. No one thinks today is a good day to overdose on any kind of drug. People clear on where they're going or what they're bringing don't establish relationships where they're bullied or become the bully. This is not the reality. When we find our purpose, we can recalibrate those choices and those events. We can decodify what really happened and redirect our new intention of helping others. These things can be used to positively fuel the future.

I'm not talking about paying off karmic debts and being racked with shame or guilt. What I'm saying is you can rebalance the impacts you've had and cast a new shadow with greater depth and a lasting reach that helps others simply because this is fulfilling. It adds wealth to others; mentally, physically, emotionally and spiritually depending on your persuasion.

With purpose as a compass your actions will hold a deeper resonance and level of significance. As you develop the skillset and heart-set it will continue the shift to purposeful.

Much like felling trees, we sometimes feel like the tree being dropped and sometimes as the lumberjack with the axe, in truth we are often both at the same time.

We feel like the tree crashing to the ground in horrific splendour, we feel like the world is taking us out at the knees. Anguished and bereft from our environment, disconnected, hurt and dying.

Yet at other times we glory in being the axe swinger, creating the fuel to sustain our family through the winter yet to come. We swing the axe magnificently, split logs and keep everyone safe and warm over the freezing months.

How we choose to look at every event is our choice – the events that have been done cannot be changed, they can only be reinterpreted.

Last year's felled tree is next year's fuel. Those events that came before are simply events – how you look at them and what you do with them is purely a matter of understanding. Are you fell or is it fuel?

If you feel dropped where is the fuel? What about it can ignite you further?

What is it that stopped you in your tracks? What is it you lacked that stopped you dead and what is it you can give to bridge that gap for others?

3. Where your 'Purpose' can take you has nothing to do with your background or perceived standing in your current community.

Although your 'Purpose', in part will be an element of nature, produced in part by the impacts of the environment on your forefathers and mothers.

Those surroundings, those elements will not define what you can do with that purpose. Many rich people have come from incredibly poor backgrounds, many adverse conditions have created phenomenal results.

True, not everyone does. Not everyone has the insights shared in order to catalyse that moment into an incredible future. There is a learning process in play that continually over lays through each event and each generation and once we see the learning, we can shift the outcome.

Your family background or standing in your direct surroundings does not shape what you do and how you focus your purpose. Like anything we experience, it is a reference point, a platform, not a mill stone.

You cannot blame your parents or your surroundings for what you choose to do with those things or how you choose to react to them. Clarity of purpose helps you to make the best out of every situation. We are not defined by our environment; we define our environment by what we put into it.

WE ARE NOT DEFINED BY OUR ENVIRONMENT; WE DEFINE OUR ENVIRONMENT BY WHAT WE PUT INTO IT

4. It helps you to set your priorities in life and identify what is really important and what isn't. It's a guide and a moral compass.

It gives you clarity of action. It causes you and encourages you to ask; is what I'm doing meaningful and purposeful?

Am I fulfilled when I do these things or, do I feel empty when I don't?

Some people naturally know their calling and go whole heartedly into doing these things – because it's instinctual. Still, many of us do what we're taught or told to. When we have it, when we feel it, we will prioritise actions that make us feel these things and also prioritise events that enable us to ignite those feelings in others.

With purpose we will actively reorder, recalibrate and refocus our days to make sure they're full of purposeful action in service to others.

"YOUR DEGREE OF FULFILMENT IS GOING TO COME FROM YOUR DEGREE OF FOCUS"

CALVIN WITCHER -

Through the lens of your 'Purpose' you will begin to understand what is trivial. When reviewed, we will find the relevant and significant and eliminate those previously perceived blockers immediately knowing that when they're cleared, we can focus our attention into greater pieces of work. They become stepping stones rather hindrances.

The other aspects that we truly cannot tolerate, or even despise – these will not be in line with our 'Purpose'. This latter part will be hinged on 2 dynamics –

i.   Ethically, from an organisational view point, does the company you work for, or the industry you're in, align with your personal values? Does it support you creating the impact you are designed to create in the world? If not, you will feel a steady drip of anxiety and depression that builds over time. A physical nudge to move.

ii.   Actions that are pulling you away from where you're "meant" to be. There will be a push/pull of what you feel like you're doing and what you're being 'told' to do. However, if we use our 'Purpose' as a lens, we can filter this very quickly and understand actually this is a stepping stone to, or if it's a genuine retraction from where we need to be going.

Filter, focus and calibrate through it.

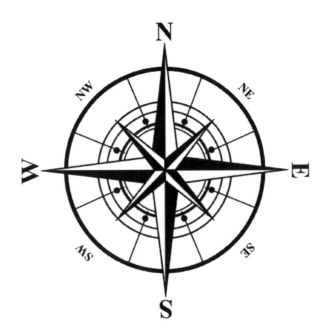

5. It helps you to structure and schedule more clearly.

As we filter our activities through our 'Purpose' and calibrate the day ahead against this, we will begin to order our actions. Prioritising and allocating the right time windows to make these happen. We will also forge through the dull and mundane tasks and activities in order to move on to more purposeful activities.

This isn't done though, in a blind fury to brush things aside, even these actions are done with intent in order to deliver in the best possible way;

A) to live up to our best version and
B) so we do not have to repeat the exercise thus wasting more time away from meaningful and purposeful work down the line.

We will allocate necessarily the right timings – chronologically and quantitively

"THE PEOPLE WHO GET ON IN THIS WORLD ARE THE PEOPLE WHO GET UP AND LOOK FOR THE CIRCUMSTANCES THEY WANT, AND IF THEY CAN'T FIND THEM, MAKE THEM"

GEORGE BERNARD SHAW -

6. It takes an accountability system to continually live it and maximise it.

Although your 'Purpose' is built in, consciously living it, is driven and learned out of you. Over the course of our growing up, through our mental and emotional development we forget to keep this at the front of our thinking.

We lack teachers at the forefront of our journey, especially in modern societal structures, we need elders and story tellers to give us a narrative to play in, up to and through.

Religion as a whole was a matter of storytelling to help keep people on track, optimally healthy - mentally and physically.

Even these doctrines are a general overview. They keep us focused as a group, with little to no shared insights into how the individualised, personal cause interlinks and lifts the group in its entirety.

The group is made up of and needs the individual. It is the same idea, the same principles that guide the collective as well as the person. Yet little focus is given to the individual.

When we learn our own language, our own reason for being here we can use this to keep the actions intentional and subsequently lift the collective. Maintaining our accountability to ourselves, as well as the tribe, it encourages us to continually live maximally in the pursuit of fulfilment at the peak of our potential. Because that's what being on 'Purpose' really is.

7. It is what you will do with joy and look forward to doing every day.

The more accountability you build into you day and the more focused that day is in delivering a service to others, the more you'll find joy in it. When you calibrate the day, the week, the month or even the year in advance, you will look forward to the activities that you are about to execute. It will bring you a sense of significance hinged on the contribution to others as you step into every eventuality

8. It helps you to identify the right partners and connection – who you need to relate to do and have in your sphere.

When we are absolutely clear on who we are and what we bring when we're at our best, whilst more clearly articulating it, the easier it is to attract the right people. It makes it easier for people to understand who you are and what you bring.

Whether this be a potential romantic partner or a future employer, it makes it vastly easier for people to fully comprehend what your values are and how you will demonstrate them in the real world.

People will be drawn to you, in order to enable you to bring more of what you believe and do to life. When your language echoes that of other organisations, especially in an interview scenario, the inevitability of securing that job increases.

"Oh, that sounds like our values"
"You'll fit right in here"
Or; *"Can we go out again?"*

On the flip side, we cannot walk into this meeting with the view point of what we want, or what we get. The moment you enter a conversation in this way, the relationship never truly clicks, never builds.

Always start conversations by expressing what you give and bring. If it's something they need then you'll collaborate, if it's not then they'll refer you to someone that does need it. Having clarity of 'Purpose' builds stronger connections.

Even the bible said;

"A MAN'S GIFT MAKES ROOM FOR HIM AND BRINGS HIM BEFORE GREAT MEN" - PROVERBS 18:16

9. In the field of your 'Purpose', you are sovereign, the director, starring role and writer.

No one else can do what you do, in the way that you do, with the inspirations that you have. No one. You are a unique combination.

Although some of your words you use may cross over with others – you are you, with your own dialogues, back stories and vehicle to present yourself.

When you're in your zone of Purpose, expertise and genius things become easier, work flows, people engage, you orchestrate the surroundings, defining your environment which in turn helps others define theirs. It gives others the inspiration to liberate their scripts and play themselves more definitely.

10. It takes intentional resourcefulness to fulfill it.

Nothing can stop you when you're on 'Purpose'. When you have a cause, you'll have a more resourceful mind, you will look at things differently, you'll see solutions to every problem, rather than the proverbial problem to every solution. A new level of thinking that will mitigate risk and excitedly look for potential challenges will become apparent.

Life doesn't stop being difficult you'll simply reframe it and it'll become an opportunity to continually step up to the plate. In doing so, you'll fulfill life deliberately and no matter the challenge you will face into it completely.

You cannot activate solutional thinking while you're complaining. Seeking fulfilment and being on 'Purpose' circumvents this for you.

11. You are not really successful if you are not fulfilling it or living it

No one ever feels like they're truly making a difference unless they're living through their 'Purpose'. You'll be ticking someone else's to do list. Mentally or physically completing and fighting on someone else's agenda. It just won't feel right. When you get into that groove, where you are full and filling (full-filling) others, when you are in that space, life comes to meet you. You will go out and create rather than waiting for something to happen or worse; waiting for someone else to tell you to do something.

Success is made by the actions we take, deliberately and congruently on a daily basis. When playing this way, you will be living and loving the life you lead, because your life will be a physical manifestation of your core values and desired contribution. What is there not to love when it's a clear indication of who you are?

12. It is not something you learn in school.

Why? Many of the people in the teaching profession have not learned theirs completely. Some teachers and trainers, have subconsciously engaged with their 'Purpose' and fewer still have taken the time to learn the language of themselves in order to help deliver the greatest impact with their skills. So few have truly learned how to help others on this journey.

Those that know their calling and the field they play in, often do so unconsciously. It's what some call 'raw talent' or 'being gifted' although these individuals are an inspiration, they rarely learn how to pass the insight forward. They often lead by example and invite others to step up through their action.

Conscious, we must become.

Now, with the importance that is being applied to getting a full comprehension of your purpose, there are more resources than ever. With plenty of different courses and seminars to learn this and help you to share it more thoughtfully.

Regardless whether this is discovered through a Marketing course or through self-discovery and personal development, it doesn't matter.

Either way it's out there, waiting for you to tap into it and develop it.

What if more teachers did learn this and included elements in the way they teach to teach others?

Imagine the impact.

13. It has been in/with you all along, merely awaiting discovery.

This 'stuff' is already hardwired into your DNA, mother nature strung it there amongst the double helix of your existence.

Everything in nature has a meaning and a purpose, nothing is created as a whim. Everything in you, about you and around you is a solution to a problem. In fact, everything in nature is the solution to at least 3 problems.

Nature does everything for a reason and with purpose, nothing is wasted or obsolete – the moment something becomes obsolete it is eliminated from the chain.

14. You will have been fulfilling it without knowing.

I doubt highly there are that many people out there that consciously know that they have a purpose or even truly know what their 'Purpose' is. That number continues to decline into those that can actually articulate it clearly and demonstrate it in their actions.

Most people simply know they're not engaged with the work they do. Does this mean they know they have a purpose and are not fulfilling it or they just have a chasm or void that needs to be filled with anything?

Some of us are "lucky" to be in the right space, the right environment, getting 'spotted'. For the rest of us it's a long path of self-reflection and self-discovery.

What we like, what we don't like and what makes us feel as if we're contributing. When we find it, it is an absolute blessing needing to be channelled.

15. It may have nothing to do with your present career or the job you are doing now, yet you don't have to leave your present job or career to start fulfilling it.

When you find it, it may be directing you to something new. It may be directing you to create something more incredible and inspiring from where you are right now. It will start to illuminate the stepping stones for creating huge impact in your life and in other's.

As you start to get more clarity on your purpose and if the grand vision suddenly appears in your head. Don't worry about the 'How' and enjoy the vision. As your see the vision you'll see more steps along the way. Those stepping stones will start to have an incremental or chronological step guide to them.

When we are clear on why we do what we do, we will start to look for new opportunities where we are in our current roles.

We'll make more of the moment, rather than to moan about what is or isn't happening. We establish our stake in the ground on which we will happily demonstrate who we are to the world.

As we stake that claim, we 'll start to see the smaller steps that scale the mountain. We will be compelled not awe struck and reticent.

16. You can make a career out of it

This is huge if understood – You can have fulfilment in every day if you look for it, find it and create it.

You can focus meaningful and purposeful work in such a way it becomes a paying income stream.

As this builds momentum those next steps become clearer, like low level lighting guiding you to your destination. It will continually shepherd you forward and give you new inspirations to create more impact around you.

Then as new people come into your sphere, with new ideas and new resources the vision will expand with new avenues to deliver your 'Purpose', expanding and rolling out in front of you.

With this resulting in the ability and possibility to monetize it, create wealth and abundance, and in some cases, make you very rich – and at the same time help you to maintain your humility and focus throughout.

HUMILITY -
THE QUALITY OF HAVING A MODEST OR LOW VIEW OF ONE'S IMPORTANCE

HUBRIS -
EXCESSIVE PRIDE OR SELF-CONFIDENCE.

THE SCIENCE BEHIND PURPOSE

There is a new wave of science that now supports all the talk about Purpose and doing purposeful work. It's about time really, various authors have been talking about Purpose for about, oh say 5000 years. I, and every other author that has been presenting the case to help you clarify what and why you do what you do, is simply presenting it from a different angle for you to see the truth.

Your truth.

It so happens that this angle or that, may just be better suited to you at this point in your journey. For whatever reason, you were suddenly ready to hear it in this version. That's why you picked the book up and that's why you're reading it.

Thankfully as the science backs up the ageless wisdoms, it gets easier to present a case and help more people clarify who they are when they're at their most profound, and help them deliver more of that greatness, more of the time.

It also depends on your psychological, philosophical or spiritual persuasion. There are many steadfast atheists out there that will happily listen to Simon Sinek talk about 'Why' and plenty of Spiritualist that prefer to listen to Neal Donal Walsh.

Neither is better than the other, just a different viewing platform to the deeper truth. Regardless of how we observe something when we observe it, it becomes the reality.

What I have learned from reading these teachings and experiencing it through my life lens is this;

There is a true version of us that needs to be tapped into; re-sourced and bought to the forefront consistently in order for us to lead and create a fulfilled life. That is all.

Myself, I like to have a foot in both camps. I see the necessity for both and right now, science is starting to explain spirit. Which creates greater and easier access points.

That which has always been known is becoming undeniable through these observations and recordings.

"WHAT IF IT WERE RIGHT HERE. THAT THE BIGGEST JOYS, ADVENTURES, EXPANSION, AND PURPOSE WERE WAITING FOR YOU AS A PERSON?"

MARC-JOHN BROWN - SHAMANIC PRACTITIONER

BRAIN FUNCTIONS

If you want to get a better handle on how much fulfilment you want in your life and how to move towards 'Purposeful' work you need to start understanding how your brain is working (even just a little bit).

The first part we need to be aware of is an evolutionary sticking point in our brain functions. Referenced in countless books from medical journals to marketing psychology everyone seems to understand (needs to know) a small part of the brain mechanics that supports how we think, act and feel.

This book isn't going to be a deep dive into that, what we do need though is a high-level overview of a couple of core brain functions and where these functions occur.

The next two definitions are lifted straight out of Wikipedia;

Limbic brain –

"The limbic system supports a variety of functions including emotion, behaviour, motivation, long-term memory, and olfaction. Emotional life is largely housed in the limbic system, and it has a great deal to do with the formation of memories"

The limbic brain is where our emotions come from, and where we store learned behaviours, our core values, over time it is believed that we store our long-term memories in the emotional centre of the brain. The limbic brain also has motivations and behaviours included.

https://en.wikipedia.org/wiki/Limbic_system

Neo-Cortex –

"The neocortex, also called the neopallium and isocortex, is the part of the mammalian brain involved in higher-order brain functions such as sensory perception, cognition, generation of motor commands, spatial reasoning and language"

The first part decides how we feel – the emotional engager, the engine house and motivator/inspirator. The second then moves us towards or away from the thing that instigated the emotion for us.

Purpose is a feeling we cultivate

The limbic region is the earliest part of our brain, its core function to keep us safe and it has been primed to keep us alive – evaluating and monitoring our environment for any threat that could possibly steal our food, eat our children, or steal our mate. It does not deal in logical reason, instead works on instinct and reflex. Not language and reasoning.

No one reasons with a person attempting to eat their children.

Through evolution as mammals we have learned what is a threat and through pleasure and pain receptors what to move towards and move away from. Instinct.

This is why when we are born, we're only born with 2 fears already baked in;

A) Loud noises and B) Falling.

https://en.wikipedia.org/wiki/Neocortex

Over a course of thousands, if not millions of years, we have learned that both these things represent danger, pain, separation and possible death for self or others.

Through emotional responses to these we have learned to avoid them and coded them into the deeper parts of our brain.

Through repetition, evolution has taken over and this has been passed on to the next generation to help avoid wasting time in the learning process. Storing it deep in the limbic system, building it as a habit in the Basal Ganglier - It's a safety mechanism enabling human development and the continuation of the species by passing on evolved behaviours.

It reduces the learning time and helps the species survive.

No different from baby birds fleeing cats.

Instinct, not reasoning.

The addition of the neocortex, approx. 200,000 years ago, gives us the ability to dissect our behaviours, rationalise our values and stimulate emotion outside of a real event.

The limbic system cannot differentiate between real or recollected. A thought raises an emotion in order to prepare a necessary reaction regardless of the reality of where we are. We can think of a physical fight we had at school, or a conversation we're about to have and adrenaline will flood the system in anticipation or remembering. How many times have we thought about something and as a result screwed up our face and started reciting what you wanted to say?

The emotions are real and the thoughts imagined.

The Limbic system simply cannot compute, in the animal kingdom. Animals don't have this because they don't have neocortices to think about things in this way. They just are right where they are, it's not the done thing for a Hyena or Zebra to worry on possibilities, they deal with actualities.

Natural presence not imagined moments.

Everything filters first through the limbic system, before it reaches the upper regions of the brain. Those that have a better self-awareness understand this and take the lead on their emotions first rather than letting their emotions run them. We channel the thinking to seek beneficial feelings and emotions, approach things logically and feel more clearly. They clarify the appropriate emotions rather than opening the flood gates to a huge cocktail of brain chemistry that could lead us everywhere but where we need to be.

We have to find a healthy balance – a combination of both elements.

Logic and feelings.

Too far one way and we end up like Vulcans from Star Trek, swing the other way and we end up as a bunch of wishy-washy hippies on a love fest putting flowers in gun barrels to create world peace.

The challenge is that the limbic system is where you and your deepest values are. In this space there are no words, so what we do is express ourselves the best we can through our actions, and hope others understand what we're doing. Sometimes this works and other times we miss by a country mile.

When we learn to speak the right words and express his through our actions people will get it, the video and the audio will sync up.

People will get you and will look to support you because each piece of information they are receiving resonates and connects. Like a branding exercise for a company, does the message link up with the product and then link to the customer service provided?

When each element is aligned people will want to connect, the transition becomes easier to move down and the path is clearer. They will feel you emotionally and will look to connect with you. When they see the emotions you evoke in yourself when you're on Purpose and serving a cause greater than yourself – they will magnetize to you.

In order to do this, we need to isolate the actions, the contribution that brings us the greatest joy and sense of fulfilment in what we do. We need to create a 'Purpose Statement' that channels our thinking and our words.

A CONVERGENCE OF IDEAS -

Let me share where this idea has grown from first of all.

This is the expansion of 2 different ideas.

I am.

There is no more powerful statement in our language, in any language, than 'I am'.

Whatever you follow this with is a given, it rapidly becomes the reality and whether you're saying consciously or unconsciously it is a choice of words that becomes pervasive in your life. A primary focus, that if repeated in multiple moments is perceived as permanent.

Let me put it in print here again -

What you think of yourself is what you'll achieve.

We start our sentence, we drop whatever we think we are in at this point, more over we drop in what we hear or believe others think we are.

We choose and learn to believe what we hear repeatedly and whatever emotions come along with this. Over the course of time we've heard these statements we attach the emotions to go them in spades.

At this point it become like a game of emotional Buck-a-Roo. The game with the plastic Mule, being loaded with more and more items. Our emotions represented by a hat, a rope, or plastic pick or pack.

As we keep piling on the emotional weight with the 'I am', we've learned to believe we are the tension builds, until we hang one more item on the little plastic Donkey only to have it buck so violently that every part of the so-called emotional stability that has been constructed is completely shattered and what is left is, by appearance, just a big mess.

As children, we would excitedly pick up the pieces to play again. As adults, working with our emotions, we do everything we can to hold the Donkey together so we don't have to deal with the mess. It always seems like the worst part; picking up the scattered pieces.

What very few people will tell you though is that you can change the label at any point, tear it off, start again and rewrite it. And we can, whenever we want.

What you say becomes a truth.

Choose and re-choose your words on a regularly basis.

Let me remind you as I was told *"Labels are velcroid, not super glued"* – Peter Sage.

As I was taught early in my personal development journey in Goal setting – you always start your goal with 'I am' they're always in the present tense. In the actual, in the real.

"ONCE YOU LABEL ME YOU NEGATE ME."
– SØREN KIERKEGAARD

The 'Why'

Since 2012 I have been digging into my reason for being, my 'Why' my purpose.

With Poppy, my daughter, due to arrive in the December of that year I wanted to know who I am, truly. And also, with the impending challenge of parenthood who I was in relation to her and in the grand scheme of things. This is where Simon Sinek popped up, fortuitously. This is where the idea of a 'Why' came up, a structure to isolate a reason for existence, my existence yet more importantly how that impacts others.

Studying Simon's work and course he spoke of his idea around the 'Why' and creating a 'Why' statement;

To...
So That...

'To' being the contribution, an action we do and the reason that we exist.

In short, my/your reason for being here is 'To' do XYZ.
In writing this though, in this way I found it was missing a level of urgency and necessity, it still held a possibility of option. You could do it or not do it if you wanted to. Or so it felt.

Even though you know this is you at your best you didn't have to actually take the action. As I've said before in here humanity cannot afford any half measures or dabblers – it needs the focused version of you, doing your version of incredible and changing lives for the better. Not just being aware of your greatest version, or the thing that you love doing when you're in this zone, but someone that actually takes the realisation and realises it.

Fast forward a handful of years to 2018.

I got to meet Peter Sage, the man that sparked my thinking into gear to become some sort of entrepreneur and nudged me to push myself to the upper limits of my potential.

He circled me back to the power of 'I *am*' in his 3-day Seminar 'The Sage Business School' (SBS) we spent time re-writing our own labels.

We took the time to reflect and document what we wanted to include. Changing the labels, unloading the proverbial donkey a little at a time.

The 'I am' statement as I've often seen and heard it comes across, in some cases, as too aspirational. Although immensely powerful in goal setting and creating visions of the future in your mind's eye what is it actually hinged on?

In this way it can be used as a positive affirmation; if you say it enough it'll become true because you'll believe it. But the difference between here and there is action. Just saying your aspirational 'I am' statements or goals is only a small part of the process.

The 'I am' statement has definition to it; I am this or that.

As I thought about it and began to combine the understanding of who I am when I'm at my best with the contribution that I make religiously, I started to shift the statement to a definitive thing.

Something that I embody constantly and remind myself of
at the start of each day with the intention to bring and create that throughout the day.

Something I can measure my fulfilment on.

I am... [*insert contribution*]
So that... [*created impact/growth*]

In doing this I stop it being both optional and aspirational.

I make it a necessity that I can include in my daily activity and keep it congruent with where I am now and where I am going.

"WHY WILL LIFE TEST YOU? BECAUSE THEORY DOESN'T COVER THE PRICE OF ADMISSION TO THE HIGHEST LEVELS OF BEING."

PETER SAGE -

CREATE A PURPOSE STATEMENT – 'THE LANGUAGE OF I'

It's all about the words we use and the way we focus our use of language. In creating a Purpose Statement, we can start to craft the 'Language of I' by constructing a deep 'I am' statement based on what you do when you're at your best. Not just a list of positive words and nice-to-haves, scribbled on a page.

Something that is authentically you, contributing what you do at a genetic level for the greatness of others.

We then swiftly follow the 'I am' with the 'So That...' this is the growth and impact of the 'thing' we share. The impact that your input creates.

This statement then gives us a focus point, a way to concentrate our actions into what we do at every possible juncture – every meeting, conversation, project or act of creation. It gives our aspirations clarity, it is the stuff of our core and fibre.

We use the contribution and the growth as the guiding principle for our actions, and in doing so actively seek out ways to bring the best possible version of ourselves to every event based on the emotions we connect with those behaviours.

The sooner we can reference our behaviours the sooner we can start to direct them to their fullest potential.

What we need to be able to say is;

I am...[contribution]
So that...[impact/growth]

This provides us a logical projection of the actions that stimulate the strongest emotions we love best and thrive on.

For those hardened Purpose hunters, yes, we have seen similar trains of thoughts, a culmination of a millennia in psychology has led us here. Combining this with the neuroscience, we can create very Purpose orientated action and as a species we can continue that trajectory of thought and input to the greater good of humanity all around us. On the micro or the macro.

First things first, get your 'Purpose' statement clear – understand what you're contributing and how you're positively impacting the world. Before we get into building that string of ideas.

I really want to help you see some more of the sciences behind you and your Purpose. I'm keen for you to see that, you're not some strange little happenstance or anomaly in the matrix of existence.

You have every reason to be here. It was already designed – you were asked. Your presence was requested at a genetic level to bridge some hidden need.

"Nature abhors a vacuum" and whatever that vacuum is or was when you were conceived, you're here to fill it. You must understand, whole heartedly you have a purpose and everyone and everything around you needs you to find it and be it.

"NATURE ABHORS A VACUUM"

ARISTOTLE -

EPIGENETICS

The new explorations into epigenetics and DNA are opening up new ideas and realisations of how we are wired at a biological level, which is now rubbing up against what has been known at a spiritual level for millennia.

The science is causing the left-brain thinkers to really plug into a reality of the esoteric and theologians, and the deeper the science goes, the ageless wisdoms become compounded by clearer view points, which are undeniable.

The headlines from epigenetics research – the foundation of your physical being started in the womb of your grandmother. You already existed inside the womb of your grandmother. As the foetus of your mother developed ovaries inside of her mother a complete life time of fresh eggs were created. An over stock. A woman is born with 2 million eggs in her ovaries.

Before that little girl that was due to be your mother hits puberty and even think about becoming your parent in any way shape or form about eleven thousand of those eggs die every month before this physical transition happens.

You were one of these eggs – incredible odds.

What ever happened to her, your Grandmother, physically and emotionally would have been passed on to you. The developing baby's neurons picking up on the brain chemistry being flooded into the blood stream.

The baby responding to fight or flight sensations of stressors or the calming notes of relaxing music, each feeding into the developing dynamic of the child yet to arrive.

Even the birth itself has an impact on the health of a child at a bacterial/microbial level, also the relational hormonal level and also at a DNA level. As a result, also on the egg that was scheduled to be you when that magic moment happened between mum and dad at your conception.

I say magic, and yes, I already know that you really don't want to think about 'that'. Magic because statistics that are regularly shared about the odds of you actually being here are in the high millions if not billions. Your parents meeting in the first place, their parents meeting and so on all the way back through history. On top of that during an ejaculation an average of 2-5 hundred million sperm are released.

The odds that you made it here are excruciatingly low, yet, the interesting thing is the sperm that made you may not have been the first one to arrive at the egg. The common misnomer is that it's the first sperm that races to the egg and nibbles its way through the outer egg wall and bingo the crazy sh** that is called conception happens.

Wrong. The egg chooses a sperm to start the process, it 'lets' one in.

A process sitting in the spiritual and/or in the realms of quantum biology yet still outside of our understanding.

A deeper consciousness decided to create the version of you that was most required to do what it was meant to do, equally for the highest learning of your parents, yourself and at the deepest level humanity as a whole.

There was a bigger plan.

A CHILD IS BORN

9 months later you decided to breath real air through your own lungs and crikey did you breathe it in. Like a triathlete switching from swim to run, you started the next stage of your evolution, a developmental leap and bound, lungs burning and fully kicking into gear.

All the genes in place, the initial building blocks out in the fresh air with all the senses being exposed to a plethora of data streams feeding in multiple billions of bytes of information every second onto a (fairly) blank hard drive. Patching, and developing and downloading huge swathes of information over laying this on the foundational hard coding.

Now, shift the perspective, look at a child's development from an adult view point, we've all watched developing children, whether as the parent or relative or friend of new parents we've watched as the baby developed over a course of time.

One day they look like the mother, the next like the father and then randomly they look like uncle Gustav from Switzerland who you haven't seen for 15 years. It seems to not make sense, it seems that the growing child is playing with the DNA sequencing they have, which part suits them more, how do they feel in that space, and then they shift again as their body and consciousness
develops.

There have been numerous studies across the centuries with the goal to understand personality development from Erikson's Psychosocial Developmental Theory to Piaget's Cognitive
Developmental Theory with numerous others developing these thoughts in many ways.

Regardless, what I know from having become a parent and observed it with my own eyes, the instantaneous behavioural shifts in a growing baby are mind blowing.

One day you're saying they are their mother's daughter, the next it's their father's daughter. Yet, the next day you're saying "where did that come from?"

These are the combination of inherited as well as the chosen genes kicking in physically, as well as behaviourally.

Our daughter definitely looks like her mother, the spitting image when they were the same ages, her grandmother laughs because they even did and do the same things at the same ages. Yet at the same time, she has my ears and a definite set of genes from my family that make her nose.

There are times where she is highly connected to her own emotions and others, she is a hardened little soldier in the face of adversity. Acquiring these traits from both my partner and I respectively.

There are other times she is 'her' without any inputs, uniquely herself.

Reserved and observing, learning in her own unique way.
These are the individual, personal genes included in this, that drives personal behaviour, the best parts of mama and the best parts of dada. The mix of nature and nurture with your individualism acting as the glue that binds this all together.

At the early stages of our lives we all did exactly the same thing.

INHERITED PHYSICAL IMPACTS

In December 2013 two scientist, Ressler and Dias conducted a study of inherited physical conditions. Interested by the findings that children whose parents that experienced things such as famine during World War 2 were at a higher risk of diabetes and heart conditions.

The interest pushed them to create an experiment to measure the impacts of external factors on the genetics of the offspring. In the experiment they trained mice to fear a chemical scent likened to that of cherries and almonds.

They did this by relating the smell to a low-level electric shock, high enough to hurt, low enough not to kill.

The interesting fact here, this was done to male mice only, so the genetic markers could be traced through sperm not just the embryo.

Through the course of the experiment the mice associated the smell with the pain and eventually began to shudder at the smell even without any shock occurring. As such, the learned behaviour was deeply encoded through the connection of neural pathway also known as the myelination process. This connection and embedded of thinking illustrated and highlighted Heb's Law which states – *"Neurons that fire together wire together"*

The study showed that the reaction was passed on to the mouse pups.

Although never exposed to the shock outcome related to the original smell, when they encountered the chemical scent, they showed a fearful reaction to the smell. The extension of the previous thought – Neurons that fire together, wire together – they also sire together.

This is evolution at its best.

These specific, lifesaving instincts are then inherited. Evolution at work in order to enable a survival of a species, the species that learns quickest keeps procreating. Yet, surprisingly, in the study they found that the learned behaviour continued on to the grandchild of the original mouse, the fear was passed forward two generations.

Like a row of dominos, before the first domino lays flat, it has already handed forward the kinetic energy to knock over another 2-3 more dominos and created the impetus to knock over the next however many dominos are in the line of succession.

Yet even in writing this a question came up for me. Although the new behaviour is wired in and handed down and dissipates over time, does that mean that although the behaviour lessens, is it easier to invoke that feeling in a future generation than others not versed in that experience?

Right now, at 40 years old, I have been impacted physically and emotionally by activities from World War 2. Whether this be austerity measures taken by my grandparents through that era, or even by those fighting on the front lines. Those carrying undisclosed PTSD and undealt with traumatic events have handed down behaviours at a cellular level. This is only now being understood through epigenetics. Does the result of these factors on all of us, generationally, give us a higher disposition for challenges in our mental health? It absolutely does.

They have found that certain people do have a higher disposition for specific mental health challenges.

https://www.ncbi.nlm.nih.gov/pmc/articles/PMC5573560/

As well as the previously highlighted physical health challenges. If the environment is just right this can trigger a reaction which presents through one of the myriads of mental health cases and variations that we regularly see in modern society.

No, this isn't a thread to hang an excuse on, because we always, always have a choice in every moment of what we want to make happen.

Granted, we may not fully understand that at the time. What it is, is helpful in understanding a mechanical prevalence for something that causes a chemical response in the brain. In this we can counter it by stimulating and introducing the chemicals that keep us moving forward rather than hold us back.

There are various steps and processes available now, and the clearer we are on how it works and what we can do with it, the easier it is to then get a much firmer handle on the horrendous and crippling experiences that can occur as a result of these mechanics and ways of thinking.

Is it simple? No, it is not.

Is it repairable? I believe it all is.

"YOU ALONE ARE THE ARCHITECT OF YOUR EVOLUTION" - RICHARD RUDD

Exercise –

We want to be able to start getting a view point on what it is we're designed for. What we came here to do.

We can already start creating this clarity by starting to look at what our parents gave us and taught us. When we can see the benefits and value in this it becomes much easier to make good use of it. Rather than blaming them we can celebrate what it enables in us.

Get 1 A4/A3 sheet; turned landscape. See Pg 143 for an example.

Break it down into 4 columns –

Title column 1; What did I Inherit and/or Learn

Title column 2; From - Mum/Dad. Can also include primary care givers and/or grandparents etc. (this column can be quite slim)

Title Columns 3; How it helps or has helped?

Title Column 4; How would I like to replace it? Or what else can I do now to use it positively?

Depending on your relationship with your family this may raise a number of emotions. We need to be mindful of this and remain as objective as possible and that involves focusing our questions and keeping them fixed on the positive outcome and not getting embroiled in the emotional maelstrom that can sometimes be family life.

This is not an exercise in blame, not about playing victim or persecutor. This is about the analysis in order to start unpicking what you're good at and what is You at your core.

Column 1 – Skills/Traits

List everything you inherited genetically, mentally and physically from your family.

Everything; tall, short, athletic ability, book smarts, game smarts, business smarts, habits (all of them). There are no good or bad in this. It is just reporting, zero judgement.

As an example, even Marianne Faithfull admitted that she *"would be dead"* without heroin. For her, it was what kept her alive and moving forward at that point in her life.

Other people reading this may have started smoking or drinking because of a parent. There is a multitude we can pick up and learn along the way. What we think maybe be bad definitely has something to be seen and valued in it.

Like I say - zero judgement. This list is just for you, not for sharing.

We need to make it as objective as possible. Just a list of words talking about elements you received as a result of being born and living where you lived and grew up.

Remember they (as well as you) did the best they could with the best they had at the time.

"THE GOAL ISN'T TO BE SOBER. THE GOAL IS TO LOVE YOURSELF SO MUCH THAT YOU DON'T NEED TO DRINK." - UNKNOWN

Column 2 - Who From?

Clarify who did you learn it from; straight forward. Again, no blame. You can use this information at a later date to potentially decipher why they may have done this or acting in such a way. It may open up the internal dialogue to go and find out and heal any unresolved hurts.

Column 3 - How has it helped you?

It's easy for me to say with my inherited height (6'6") that I can help little old ladies in super markets reached the last box of cereal, or find someone in a crowded bar. Shortness has its virtues.

Blonde, Red, White, Black whatever it may be, how has what you've inherited genetically helped you?

Not, how has it hindered you or held you back? How has it helped you, kept you alive, saved you from shi**y relationships? Whatever it might be we're looking for the discernment and the uplifts here.

When I was young, I was a bit awkward, and some girls used my height as an excuse not to go out with me. Looking back now,
I can say brilliant! Definitely don't need people in my life like that –
back then it made me feel uneasy and unlikeable.

Now, I've celebrated my height through my martial arts, developed my presence as a trainer and speaker. It definitely is a gift. Seeing it this way now is going to help my 6-year-old daughter grow up comfortable in her skin. Currently wearing 9-year olds clothes, I can and will help her bridge this future learning sooner and embrace who she'll become with her confidence and her presence.

Also, think about the mindsets you learned, coping mechanisms, approaches to life. Who did you get them from and how have they helped you?

Like the mention of Marianne Faithful earlier; even our addictions, are coping mechanisms, are a strategy to keep us from tipping completely over the edge at times. They served a purpose.

It's about looking at the things we've done and seeing how they helped us or moved us forward.

Remember; Non-Judgement.

What we can start to realise as we're doing this is; that yes, these things have kept us alive and got us this far, it may be time now though to tweak and adjust them.

It could well be the time to stop some of them altogether and try something new to raise the game further. This is an opportunity to say thank you to those habits and behaviours that now need to change and become something else.

Seriously, take a moment to say thank you to those things that have served you this far, but are now doing you a dis-service and are holding you back.

"I just want to take this moment to say thank you to my [insert habit/mind set], you're help has been greatly appreciated in my life, now I need to do [insert new habit of mindset] to help me move forward on my journey."

If you need help to do this, then find the right coach, mentor or counsellor to do this. If you've found something you would like to change then this is a great opportunity to start the next stage of learning – do it!

How else does this help? By doing this exercise we're already starting to collate words that we can use in our Purpose Statement. It's starting to focus our thinking on the things we do when we're at our best and the impacts we want to create with them.

And remember, no one wakes up and thinks; "Today I'll be an ar$ehole" This exercise is to help us to start addressing what we're doing, why we're doing it and how we can improve it further.

That's all, it's a learning process to build things up, learn, refine and improve. It's a growth centric experience.

Column 4 – How would I like to expand or replace it?

Here's the opportunity to grow or rewrite the future. You've highlighted what has worked, and potentially what may not be serving you.

In this column you can ask yourself what do I need to do now to move me to the next level or to evolve further to create more fulfilment?

This last part starts to point the thinking in a new direction.

What I learned or Inherited	Who from?	How did it, or does it help?	How do I want to expand it or replace it?

Life as a lesson

It's simply all about Evolution; of body, mind and soul.

Psychology to physiology. It's a series of improving concepts and steps that strengthen and develop an internal and external eco-system over an extended period of time.

The way we grow is by understanding what it is we need to give and building an understanding of it and a way to bridge, a perceived gap. As parents, creating a child is one of the highest levels of learning we, as humans, can experience. In part we do this in order to reflect back on our deepest emotional gaps in order to develop forward beyond our current level of known capabilities. We create a child so we can cease thinking about ourselves and pour our attentions and affections in to a joint creation of 2 people culminating from and in a physical and emotional union. We are hardwired to be selfless and serve others. That's the core emotional concept behind procreation.

As a child you have already had a purpose installed. It comes as a factory default, built in you and for you to help the learning of your parents, they created you to learn more about life as a larger whole. They have given you the mirror to reflect back to them that which they need to see. Did you ever wonder why your relationships with your parents can be so challenging?

This learning you're providing them is also echoed out to help others, beyond your family into your community and the people you connect with. Again, building their experiences in order for them to grow emotionally and spiritually. In reciprocity, your parents will pass on their learnings also, building and challenging your understanding. Others will see this; will see how you evolve and it encourages them to grow also. We teach through our actions more than our words.

That is the lesson you share outwardly. The lesson you build inwardly come as a reflection on and of what you project outwardly. By understanding what we cause and create we learn from this echo. Like sonar bouncing back to us as feedback, showing us a picture. It enables us to step up a gear when we build this understanding of ourselves in the physical world. The clearer the image we get, the easier it is for us to magnify our growing experiences.

- What did we do?
- What was the result?
- How do improve this?

We have to be growth centric. Progressively orientated.

The idea is to raise your self-awareness and take a higher level of responsibility in order to create stronger outcomes for those you interact with.

"A *rising tide lifts all boats*"

How you strengthen it is learned. What you're delivering is already pre-coded.

"BELOVED, YOUR PURPOSE IS NEVER UNKNOWN" - CALVIN WITCHER

Maybe just out of sight.

We absolutely must decipher this code; this is the route to us being on purpose. Being able to read our own matrix, understanding our own source code and unlocking the first stages of limitless potential.

MOVING INTO PURPOSEFUL

Regardless of the science; the biology, the quantum mechanics that accompany this, everyone has a purpose. Let me repeat this very, very clearly...

EVERYONE HAS A PURPOSE.

Let me give this idea a little more credibility and expand this; Reminder - Nothing in nature is created on a whim or a fancy, nothing.

Everything has a use and has its place in the grand ecology of existence. That includes every possible stretching and reaching corner of the universe. As the saying goes *"necessity is the father of invention"* (and evolution) It doesn't matter what the thing is you're looking at, you can work back to the reason and the problem.

Nature is designed that way, take a moment to look around you, look at you, look in you. Everything in you, about you and around you is a solution to a problem. Moreover, in nature things are the solution to 3,4,5 if not more things simultaneously.

Look at an Oak tree – it exchanges CO_2 for Oxygen, stores carbon, stops soil erosion, houses hundreds of species of invertebrates and others animals, produces shade creating cooler air and the list goes on.

We, as individuals, have multiple functions. Individual parts of us have multiple functions. We are hundreds if not thousands of solutions, neatly bagged up blobs of waters acting as some bipedal filter sifting through the physical and the emotional. We are designed to improve things, to solve things and to act in unison with multiple others cogs and parts. A seriously complex system.

The art in this though is to find the root first, your root. To understand what solutions, you're creating and utilise this understanding to its highest possible potential for the greater good of humanity.

No, I'm not joking.

You have the capacity to impact millions by being at your highest level of greatest good. If you so choose. You have to be aware that the only difference between a small idea and a big idea is the limit which you apply to it.

One oak tree touches every single person on this planet; billions of people breathing in the oxygen it breathes out, one acorn started it.

Let me repeat this; The only difference between a small idea and a big idea is the limit to which you apply to it.

We have to seek our version of incredible in order to reshape the future right now, we have to bring the highest possible version of us at every possible juncture. Human existence depends on it. Evolution depends on it. The first steps to incredible is first finding how you move from 'Meaningful' work to 'Purposeful' work.

How to get on, stay on and be deliberately on Purpose.

"EVERY ELEMENT HAS MULTIPLE FUNCTIONS AND EVERY FUNCTION SERVES MULTIPLE ELEMENTS"

BILL MOLLISON -

STAGE 4 - PURPOSEFUL WORK

This is when we take something that is full of 'Meaning' to us and is also full of Purpose to someone else. This is how we create 'Purposeful Work'.

The focus of the work becomes that of making others smile. We smile because they smile. The work you do becomes of service to others, it becomes dedicated to the contribution towards, and the growth of, others.

You start to understand exactly what you put into your day and you can clearly see what the outcomes of that are - it becomes selfless, community based and about building strong relationships.

The first stages of Purposeful work are about understanding what it is you do when you're at your best. Primarily how that makes you feel then redirecting that and sharing it with others.

Purpose is a feeling you cultivate and develop. You fuel it through repetition and seeking out that sensation again and again. As you seek it out further, you learn to grow it and expand it. Like the Oak tree, growing bigger, so does the impact you create as you connect more completely with your capability to help more people.

"NO MATTER WHEN OR WHERE ALWAYS BRING YOUR 'A' GAME. BECAUSE YOU NEVER KNOW WHEN IT'LL OPEN DOORS"

- SIMON SINEK

SYMPTOMS

- **Expansive -**

We look for bigger platforms and spaces to do more of this stuff and reach more people. We have to, it feels great when we do it! We begin to experience a sense of possibility, although it feels great as we impact 1 person, and even though it continues to feel great we also get a sense of desire to impact increasing numbers.

Not from a space of ego, from a space of potentiality.

- **Looking to stand out -**

Being the example and the invitation to others so they can step up. You lead the way in what you do and celebrate it by sharing it. Yet, humble enough to both let and help others step up with their own personal super powers.

- **Legacy thinking -**

You stop thinking about what you'll leave when you left, more over focusing on what continues on after you're gone. We start to think like the Greek proverb that talks about planting trees we know we won't sit in the shade of. As a result of this type of thinking, people want to be around you.

"Be the leader you wish you had" – Simon Sinek, moreover, be the leader you know the world needs. Think about the words you share and how they'll be shared in the future. That's what legacy thinking is about - every conversation, every day, week, month, year, not just vague ponderings or regrets when you're about to die.

I spent 20 years in work I was 'Told' to do. I found 'Meaningful' work at 35 and as a result it set me on the path to find 'Purposeful' work. It took about 3 years to really move into that space. I was screaming out to build on that.

I had self-reflection on my side and was able to really analyse what I was doing in speech and behaviour through my existing knowledge and skills in coaching and NLP (Neuro Linguistic Programming) The meaningful was already giving me a sensation of what was possible.

Setting myself on a path of self-determination to find more. I qualified as a Leadership Coach and Mentor, through my hours or practice to accompany the program I started to really tap into those moments of maximum contribution. Where I truly connected with another person, not for me, for them.

That's when I found something that was full of Purpose to someone else. It was when I was asking them questions that evidently raised the awareness, flicked their lights on and enabled them to drop every penny they possibly could.

Those moments, that's what creates a visceral response for me.

That, to me, is my version of fulfilment.

Chills in the face, goose bumps across my arms. The thrill that this person I'm now giving to is tapping into their version of incredible, and although I had been doing it a little whilst doing meaningful work, this now opened the doors to a whole new world of possibility. Not just for me, or the single client, for what I later came to understand as potentially the whole world.

There is a version of this that is yours.

GIVING IS GOOD FOR YOU

Being of purpose and doing purposeful work isn't just a fitting morale to an Aesop fable that helps us to be a better human being. It's science-fact that it's good for you and those around you. If you need more convincing of the cognitive benefits, with modern technology, that which has been professed, documented and iterated is now being backed up with the Newtonian psychological and physiological sciences.

Publicised May 2016, and demonstrated with the use of fMRI (functional magnetic resonance imaging) lead researchers; Tristen Inagaki, PhD, of University Pittsburgh and Naomi Eisenberger, PhD, of University of California, Los Angeles demonstrated the importance of giving support and of being a contributory factor in your space and community.

The study included 36 subjects from a larger study of the "neural mechanisms" of social support. Further distilled to; the changes within the brain that may explain the reduction in stress and other health-promoting effects of support (given and received).

Those taking part as subjects were asked to remember and think about time where they either had "someone to lean on" or were "looking for ways to cheer people up" when they are feeling down. Consistent with previous studies, "Both receiving and giving more support were related to lower reported negative psychosocial outcomes" the Doctors said.

This was then broken down 3 further ways whilst being scrutinised by the fMRI to explore which parts of the brain was involved in; stress-, reward-, and caregiving-related activities versus receiving social support which clearly showed activation of specific brain areas in response to different types of tasks. In all three activities studied, the scans showed brain activation that correlated with individual differences in giving support, but not receiving it.

For example, while performing a stressful mental math task, participants who reported giving the most support had reduced activation in brain areas related to stress responses. In contrast, receiving a lot of support was unrelated to activation in stress-related regions.

The results questioned the conventional idea that the health benefits of social support mainly reflect received support.

"At the level of the brain, only support giving was associated with beneficial outcomes," according to Doctors; Inagaki, Eisenberger and co-authors.

But, the importance of understanding, knowing and focusing your contribution is absolutely tantamount to reap the full benefits of this.

Dr Inagaki and a different team; Lauren P. Ross, BA, of University of Pittsburgh, in their research paraphrased here explain how important specific giving is, and also how crucial the tangibility of this to those health implications.

"ONLY SUPPORT GIVING WAS ASSOCIATED WITH BENEFICIAL OUTCOMES"

- DOCTORS; INAGAKI, EISENBERGER AND CO-AUTHORS.

https://www.sciencedaily.com/releases/2016/02160211184959.htm

https://insights.ovid.com/article/00006842-201605000-00007

A few months later, in October 2018, confirming a new level of depth to this and compounding a deeper understanding, when we give what was referred to as "untargeted" support and/or giving ie passing charity giving. The good deed simply does not have the same neurobiological effects.

"Our results highlight the unique benefits of giving targeted support and elucidate neural pathways by which giving support may lead to health" they wrote.

Performing a pair of experiments to evaluate brain responses to providing different kinds of social support. In the first study, 45 volunteers performed a "giving support" task where they had a chance to win rewards for someone close to them who needed money (targeted support) against; for charity (untargeted support), or, finally, for themselves.

As predicted, participants felt more socially connected, in my words 'Purposeful', and felt that their support was more effective, when giving targeted social support. In short it would be tangible and palpable as it related to someone or thing that was connected to them.

Following this, the subjects then underwent an emotional ratings task including fMRI scanning to assess activation of specific brain areas when giving social support.

Providing support, regardless of who received the support, was linked to increased activation of the ventral striatum (VS) and septal area (SA). These are the areas of the brain previously linked to parental care behaviours in animals.

However, only higher activation of the SA when people gave targeted support was associated with lower activity in the amygdala – that amazing piece of hardware often related to fear and stress responses.

In short "*Humans thrive off social connections and benefit when they act in the service of other's well-being,*" according to the authors. The new study adds further evidence that giving specific, focused support may be uniquely beneficial.

Both targeted and untargeted support are linked to increased positive brain functions (SA/parenting activity), supporting the "warm glow" theory of providing support: we help others, directly or indirectly, simply because it feels good it is meaningful and purposeful and feel good hormones get released, health benefits prevail and the desire to repeat kicks in.

But, in order to create the long-standing benefits of community building, relationship nurturing and personal health generative – it's got to be aligned, specific and targeted, not just a cursory flinging of change into a pot. Although the coin tossing is good it's just not long lasting.

It's all about the connection.

Your solution is unique and specific and has to be directed and utilise in this way in order to create fulfilment.

To do that, for most people it takes a little self-discovery.

"...AND BENEFIT WHEN THEY ACT IN THE SERVICE OF OTHER'S WELL-BEING"

- DOCTORS; INAGAKI AND CO-AUTHORS.

https://www.sciencedaily.com/releases/2018/08/180830125128.htm

https://insights.ovid.com/crossref?an=00006842-201810000-00006

UNCOVER YOUR PURPOSE -

Countless times I've heard people talk about getting mentors and teachers and saying things like "Success leaves clues".

Correct success does, what is often missed and far more important - you left clues.

"AN UNEXAMINED LIFE IS NOT WORTH LIVING"
- SOCRATES

What you must remember, keeping the idea that you've left success related clues in mind, is that you have to become aware of the fact that you have already clearly illustrated what your purpose is through your interactions in multiple previous scenarios. In fact, near every interaction.

Now, it is now time to find and tap into those clues in order to help yourself start finding meaning in what you're doing. Purely, with the intention of finding ways to create more of that in your day, not for you, for those you engage with in future interactions.

TIME TO START PLAYING TRICKS ON YOURSELF

To do this we need to deconstruct some of the events in your life, we need to dig about in them and start finding some commonalities in your choices of language, choices of reaction and response. We need to start seeing what you bring when you're at your best and even sometimes when you're at your, so-called worst.

These choices are defined in moments of truth. Moments when you have no choice, you cannot faulter in your action because the action is taken out of your mind and delivered from a clearer state of consciousness. From something contained and harboured in you at that genetic level. It is your instinctual response – that one that is unique to the evolutionary steps that created this you, in this moment. The solution.

You will do what you have been wired to do. It is not learned, it is part of the operating system you arrived with. External forces cannot change it, you at your deepest is always present. The external environment can direct it or bend it. It can give you tools and viewpoints to overlay on it.

Regardless it can never break it or reshape it, it will always be a guiding principle in your activities for good or for bad. Yet the beauty of our minds is, which we must be aware of when doing this, when we go back and think about these events and moments, we summon up the same, if not intensified sensations and feelings.

As much as they act as reminders of what made the event so important.

It's vital to comprehend how the body responds physiologically near exactly the same if you simply remember the same situation, or even imagine a future similar event.

We have to remember - In summoning action replays based purely on imagination, we can induce stress hormones through thought alone. A phenomenon that can both plague us if we remain anchored in the past or get lost and anxious about the future.

If retelling some of these stories is going to uproot your past or trigger any emotional state which is going to be detrimental, please make sure you have the right people available to help you and/or do this work with a coach, mentor or counsellor with you.

Whomever has the right qualification to guide you at the right time.

Before we move into looking at these stories, one thing that might help is some understanding of how the brain is behaving, having a comprehension of what the past and the future actually are.

What you think is the past and the future, are not really what happened or are going to happen.

We need to appreciate what they are so we can gain the advantage from these thoughts. Then we can start to create the objectivity required to retrieve what we need to extrapolate from them.

"THE QUESTIONS YOU ASK YOURSELF WILL DETERMINE THE COURSE OF YOUR LIFE"

TOM BILYEU -

The Past –

The past is a present-day recollection of a previous event with your imagination filling in the blanks and your emotions escalating or smoothing over key elements.

The Future –

The future is a present-day imagining of an event yet to take place with your imagination filling in most of the yet to be, and your emotions escalating key parts based on your present-day experiences of previous events.

"I HAVE REALIZED THAT THE PAST AND FUTURE ARE REAL ILLUSIONS, THAT THEY EXIST IN THE PRESENT, WHICH IS WHAT THERE IS AND ALL THERE IS." - ALAN WATTS

Both of which lead to stifled potential, hobbled capabilities and in the end anxiety and depression.

Yet at the same time with some objectivity we can use this brain trickery to our advantage. We can learn lessons about ourselves and start to uncover the operating system, learn the source code and create more dynamic future scripting.

When looking for 'Purpose' what we need is to find those feelings, find the actions, those things you did that stimulated the emotions that went with it.

MOMENTS OF TRUTH

We use these previous moments and we create new, freshly empowered ones moving forward.

What we can also do is leverage imagined events. In bringing these to mind we place the mind under an interesting illusion in itself to get a deeper view of itself, now or in the future and mostly when you're at your best.

In order to start formulating the language of Purpose we need to retrieve our moments of truth, either passed or yet to come. Thinking about this, what is the biggest moment of truth in your life? The day you meet your partner, your wedding day, a child's birth?

The single biggest moment of truth you have in your life is still yet to come. There is only one – it's the day you die.

There is nothing so full of truth than that moment just before you leave. Nothing to hide, no win, no lose. Just a moment to reflect instantaneously before you, in this form, pass.

It is the time you look back and decide if you filled your life with everything you meant to do, or did you waste it worrying about and/or doing pointless sh*t?

Tough question. Not one that I would ever apologise for. You, we all need to think about this stuff.

Doesn't matter how old you are. You need to bring it to your awareness and get conscious of it. Death is a given, inescapable.

Because the moment you start to see the world through this truth you will start acting as though life is important. You're important and mostly what you do with it is very, very important. You need to fill your life with incredible stuff that is fulfilling to you and others in a way that only you know how to do.

As I said, nature creates everything for a reason, that includes you.

A previous client told me that as a *"modern society we have become death-phobic."*

We ignore what is, at this time of writing this, a guaranteed event.

"Death is the dark backing that a mirror needs if we are to see anything" wrote Saul Bellow.

It is not a sad moment, it's a close of a chapter. A moment to review and celebrate.

And as Stephen R Covey said in *'The 7 Habits of Highly Effective People'*

"BEGIN WITH THE END IN MIND"...

...and this is the biggest end we can tangibly perceive. When we look at the world from this point and with the inevitability of death, we create a certain stability in our thinking, we shape a deeper view point on what we're here to bring. We get a fresh clarity of our daily actions and they make a newer, crisper note of resonance.

We will take a fully ownership of what we were given at birth and create an authorship of the chapters yet to be written right up to that final sentence.

When you get this thought in your thinking more regularly you will squander fewer days on pointless, or in the worst case, hurtful and toxic activities. You will look to add more value, because it will align with the vision you have of your final day.

Look at it from a different angle and in doing so start to map forward so you can engineer backwards. You can take a moment right now to recount your life, the life you most deeply want to shape and bring to fruition, with the intention of making it really count, not for you, for those that matter.

"DEATH IS THE DARK BACKING THAT A MIRROR NEEDS IF WE ARE TO SEE ANYTHING"

SAUL BELLOW -

'PERCEPTUAL POSITIONING' – THE CONCEPT OF WHAT WE'RE ABOUT TO DO HERE.

A technique taught through NLP and made good use of by coaches and great leaders alike. I wanted to share this now as this is the core concept for viewing the world celebratory, from your death bed. It also has great value and is an awesome tool to use in many job roles and moments to help raise awareness from different viewpoints. Worth keeping in the tool box outside of this context – as a leader also as a parent.

Here's an over view, then after we'll apply this to finding purpose.
The concept enables an individual to change their view point and as a result think about things from a different perspective. The human brain being what it is has a malleable frame of reference which can be consciously shifted to that of other people and also of others times and places.

Here's an example of how it can be used.

Take a situation at work. Any situation that has happened or is poignant to you.

You can already see this from your own perspective, your personal, first player vantage point.

What happened?
What did you see and do? What would you do differently?

Now mentally change your position. Change it to that of your manager.

What do or did they see?

As if you're them, what do you think of the situation?

What would they suggest to do next time to improve it further?

Now shift again.

- What about the view point of the customer or end user?
- What do they see?
- What would they like to experience differently next time?
- What would they like to happen next time to create a more holistic outcome?

Now you have some new view points of the same situation from different perceived positions. You have a handful of new expectations and ideas that would improve the outcomes for those external viewpoints.

The interesting part here though, we have to internalise those new views. Without bringing them back to your own thoughts they quickly dissipate as they are un-associated to you. You have to change position and close the mental loop by coming back to first player mode and then associate and incorporate the new thoughts.

We do this by focusing the new thoughts through questions -

"From what I have seen, what can I incorporate next time that will improve my delivery?"
"What 1 thing did I just experience that I can do right now to push this and me forward?"

Now the actions are personally associated, they belong to you and are owned, not just a perceived idea.

How can we make use of this when comprehending our 'Purpose'?

DEATH BED

To some this may feel like a sad experience. Having delivered this in numerous 1-2-1 and group conversations, for some this does bring up tears. We often don't want to think about dying, if we want to design and deliver incredible - we have to it.

This isn't about making you feel sad; this is about opening your eyes and get clearer and create more smiles by doing more of the things you're about to see. We have to understand that dark backing to the mirror, then we'll see all of life reflected in the mirror we want to be looking into.

With absolute love and respect and a privilege that I always feel when I walk people through this, I invite you to start walking this train of thought to help open your eyes further.

Grab a pen and your notepad – they'll be some questions to ask in your imaginings shortly and you'll need to write these answers down.

NB Remember, it is important to answer these as your older self, the leader and leaver of the fullest life you can imagine having completed. Not as the person you are right now, saying things like "I hope I" or "I think I would have"

Answer everything as the 100-year-old version of you. What did you do, what did you say, what actions did you take all those times?

Write every thought down you can bring to memory and write them as your future self.

Also note, when writing any of your stories down or key elements, write single sided, don't use both sides of the page, there may be a need to see all the details in one space and having to flip them over will just be a barrier.

This is day zero, the clock counted down.

You made it to the end. Congratulations.

DAY ZERO

Exercise –

Close your eyes and imagine this scene –
You're lying on your death bed. You're ready to leave. You've led an incredible life, you filled it full of good and great things. Your body is older than you could have imagined and your eyes are still full of vitality – because you made every day count.

You're surrounded by family; they know as well as you that the time has come. Your children, you're grandchildren even. Maybe the Children of close friends that call you aunty or uncle are there. It is sad, for them but they are so blessed to call you by the cherished name they call you. You've done everything you possibly could to light up their worlds and teach them how to light up others.

For you, you have nothing to do except rejoice in the life you've lived. I feel blessed to share this moment with you, as a friend. It is incredible to see so many amazing people coming to you right now to say good bye. At the same time, I need to know some answers about you to share with others once you leave so I can share your insights on to the next generation.

Looking back on your life right now, from your final resting place answer me these questions;

Action –

Make sure you write down each answer, spend as much time as you need to on each, get the pen to paper and write, and don't stop writing until you feel you've exhausted your thoughts and beyond, you are writing about a life yet lived and yet already done, so fill it up with magnificence

Tell me;
- At the end of your life what is it that you most proudly achieved or accomplished?
- What do you most regret not having done?
- What matters most to you?
- What was it you did that brought you the most joy?
- How did you teach this to others?

Take your time and write down everything that comes to mind.

MATERIAL OVER IMPACT

If you have written fiscal details here – amounts of money, nice house, fast car here's the rub. Honestly, how quickly will these things be forgotten once you're gone? Whether you owned a house or not, or what that house really looked like no one will really care, the money in the bank account will become someone else's.

Another number on another month end statement.

Go into your questions, get back on that bed –
- What is it you want to be truly remembered for?
- What positive attributes do you want your family to remember you for when you're gone?
- What is it that will continue on, after you're gone?
- What will be remembered?

Here's an example of 'Result over Legacy';

'The Battle of Greatness'

Love him or hate him the Floyd Mayweather, as seen on television, will only be remember for a limited amount of time for a limit number of things.

Most of those things will be related to numbers – monetary results and a level of self-absorption and arrogance that goes with this. I say this from a view point of his media persona, whether this is true or not I cannot say. I think the media and social media feeds paint an interesting picture – one day I'm sure I'll get to find out the truth on this subject.

Yet what do we know about Manny Pacquiao, 'The Pac-Man' A quiet man in the media a great pugilist and a man of great heart.
On 2nd May 2015 these men met on the canvas and fought in 'The Battle of Greatness' as it was titled.

Pacquiao lost – 12th round, unanimous decision.

What happened after though was the interesting thing – it was what Manny did with the winnings that wasn't much discussed. At the time he was a Philippine Senator. Manny Pacquiao paid from the fight purse he secured, even though he lost, for 1,000 homes to be built for the poor in his hometown.

He was quoted as saying *"I'm so happy giving these houses free to my constituents in the Sarangani Province from my own pocket – more than thousand families are the beneficiaries,"* he posted on Facebook.

What will be remembered? A photo of a man in a limo holding lots of money or the love and generosity that was shared for those families.

What will make the difference or create the impact?

WHAT HAVE YOU WRITTEN SO FAR?

As you look at the world from this point, remember these memories.

Reflect on what you've already written, what common words can you already see and read.

- What feelings came up throughout the thinking?
- What contributions did you make to the lives of those around you as they say good bye?
- What kind words do they say about you 2, 5, 10 years after you depart?
- What is it they remember fondly about you and how you helped them?

What is it you have done in this thinking that you will rejoice in at the end?

Not what you wished you'd given or hoped to do – Truly knowing you gave your everything for.

"WHEN YOU WERE BORN YOU CRIED AND THE WORLD REJOICED. LIVE A LIFE SO THAT WHEN YOU DIE THE WORLD CRIES AND YOU REJOICE."

- CHEROKEE PROVERB

Action –

You now have a series of answers, some stories and values.

Pick out the core elements, the key words, the ones that get repeated often.

What you need to be looking for is 2 things primarily –

1. Feelings
2. Actions, verbs that created these feelings

Let me say again – Purpose is a feeling you cultivate.

When you find the actions that create a certain feeling – then we're in the realms of Purpose.

My verb, my doing word is 'Challenge' for me it is about challenging peoples thinking.

Look for words that show how you've contributed and how it positively impacted others.

Also look for the results of your actions, how did others grow as a result?

Take these events apart.

LOOKING BACK FROM NOW

Now that we've looked at our life from its end, we can start to comprehend what we've done and how we've done things and continue to un-weave the lessons we've been waiting to teach ourselves.

From here, in this section, we're going to collate stories and insights from our closest past occurrences starting with the last 12 months.

NB as a leader or parent this is also a really easy approach to helping people in your family or teams to start reviewing their last year. Easy questions that really help build up a mid-year or end of year review or 1-2-1 and help them to really start investigating what they'd rather be focusing their time and energy on.

After we've looked at these questions we'll start to move back through history and see what else comes out; language wise.

THE LAST 12-MONTHS

3 QUESTIONS TO HELP GET YOU CLOSER TO PURPOSEFUL

Working in the head space of the here and now take a moment to answer these following questions on a separate piece of paper.

- In the last 12 months what events made you feel most proud at work?
- In the last 12 months what made you feel most excited in your role?
- When did you display your top 3 values that you always bring when playing at your best?

Again, write your answers down, break each story down –

- What were you doing?
- What was the actions you personally contributed?
- What did you bring?
- What was the result of those actions?
- What positive impact did you create?

Grab as many stories you can from the last 12 months, find the highest value items, the ones that caused the biggest reactions and emotional responses in you.

The ones that resonated, emotionally and viscerally.

Action –

Document all the events you can remember.

If you have them typed on 1-2-1's or Annual reviews, copy and paste them into a central place.

Ideally keep each event on a separate page, this will help later on when we bring all the stories we're starting to collate together for the latter parts of this exercise.

Put these to one side and keep them safe.

"TAKE PRIDE IN HOW FAR YOU'VE COME. HAVE FAITH IN HOW FAR YOU'LL GO."

MICHAEL JOSEPHSON -

GOING BACK A BIT FURTHER

Before we start to stretch the thinking a bit further, we're going to start pulling up some previous events; good and bad.

Why? Because these events are going to show you very clearly who you are when you're at your best and also remind you of what you need to bring when you won't so great. Either wishing you could have brought something different or someone could have brought that for you.

Again, some of these 'stories' can carry a certain amount of weight with them, some emotional baggage.

We're human, the emotions don't just leave us, or get left at the door.

It's what makes us truly human. Although seeing the wonder we've left in the world from our death bed can bring tears of joy more often than not, dealing with the last 12-months of pride and excitement don't tend to have too many challenges tagging along.

Older events may bring more with it.

Remember what I shared about the past.

It's a real time recollection of a previous event with your imagination and emotions filling in the blanks.

Most of what you think happened didn't actually happen, so we escalate and deescalate key elements depending on how we feel about them or the people involved.

The brain makes stuff up.

It doesn't help you get what you need from these moments. In the nicest possible way; remove the fluff. Get rid of the emotional wading, the stuff you've added to pack it out and justify certain reactions and behaviours.

Stripe the events back.

Hack away the unessential.

Think about the amount you add, emotionally, to events that happen in your life.

The flat tyre, the close relative that passed away, the faulty workmanship on a house repair.

As frustrating or sad as these moments can be, as human beings we spend more time embellishing extra layers over the top of events rather than processing and learning from them or celebrating them.

The brain causing distraction, justifying a behaviour, validating the reason to stay inside the comfort zone and to collude with others in order to stay put.

"You can't imagine what just happened to me..., the tyre blew, I was in the fast lane, I didn't have the jack, I was late for the interview..." so on and so forth.

Honestly, "80% of people don't care what your problem is, the other 20% are glad it's yours"

We add the filler to bring people in to our negative emotions so we can feel safe and supported. It never helps when you're in that place, how many times do you tell the same story over and over, or even have to restart the story when someone new turns up half way through.

Look at the event and ask one straight forward question - What really happened?

No filler.
No fluff.
No extra story.

What actually happened, in the least amount of words possible. You got a flat tyre and it made you later than expected. That's it. No more, no less.

What did you learn? Check the tyres more often especially on special days.

What would you do differently next time? Leave earlier, check the phone app for traffic.

The situation is teaching you and sharing wisdom, but, because of the emotional content we add, we miss the point and repeat the cycles without moving forward and this is the same for small events as with big ones.

If someone were to teach us something really helpful or share their wisdom, what's the first thing we'd say to them?

Exactly! Thank you.

Instead we dramatize the situation or give ourselves a hard time rather than simply saying thank you for the gift it's sharing.

Although, we still need to keep a level of objectivity when we do this, we can still use gratitude initially to smooth our entrance into and the handling of the thing we're reviewing. And, again if this brings stuff up, causes a reaction, then seek an appropriate support mechanism; a coach, counsellor or therapist that can point you in the right direction.

Remember this, each moment is a gift, an insight and a possible realisation about you at your absolute best. When we do this, we can get ourselves on a quest to get internal treasure that creates so much more as a result. Maximising the depth, breadth and clarity of what we do on a daily basis.

Start gathering some different items.

This next part we're going to collect are some further core stories and ideas. For each of these 3 age brackets; 25-now, 16-25 and Early years. I'm going to ask you to document 5-8 pivotal in each of those segments. The stories that have challenged you to be your most incredible or reminded you to be your greatest in the most extreme way.

For now, in each bracket, list the events simply as a title, the biggest events that come to mind in each category.

'Birth of Daughter'

'Wedding Day'

'One of my team being promoted'

'Being bullied on the way home from school'

So, on and so forth, find the ones that summon up the strongest emotional reactions (without diving into the emotions), so you know you're on the right path. Do your absolute best to keep it as objective as possible.

Remember; 5-8 stories from each section.

25-NOW

What has happened since the age of 25 that has been revelatory for you.

Good or bad, positive or negative from then to now?

Action -

List 5-8 defining moments and give each event a name and list them out.

- 1
  ....
- 2
  ....
- 3
  ....
- 4
  ....
- 5
  ....
- 6
  ....
- 7
  ....
- 8
  ....

16-24

We now understand that the human brain doesn't stop developing until around 24. Yet, unknowingly, we subject it to huge amounts of pressure in multiple forms of substance abuse. In doing so, we often collect some interesting stories from around this time of our lives.

What happened for you in this period?
What was it that happened that stands out most clearly?

Action -

Find another 5-8 events and give each event a name and list them.

- 1
  ....
- 2
  ....
- 3
  ....
- 4
  ....
- 5
  ....
- 6
  ....
- 7
  ....
- 8
  ....

What do you remember from these years? Dig up the strongest events and resonating stories you can remember from this time in your life.

Document another 5-8 events. Up's and down's, the most extreme occurrences that come to mind.

Action -

Give each event a name and list them out.

- 1

  ....

- 2

  ....

- 3

  ....

- 4

  ....

- 5

  ....

- 6

  ....

- 7

  ....

- 8

  ....

CONSTELATE THOSE ACTIONS

What does it mean to constellate?

Now we have our list we can start to map these moments together, like a star constellation, a connected pattern of occurrences.

We are 'meaning' seeking, pattern finding machines. We look at things and want to make story that can empower our thinking. Thousands of years ago we looked at the heavens and unknowing of what the stars were, began to make our own minds up and filled the sky with stories and gods of every creed and belief.

But until we did that, they were individual dots of light in the darkness. Then, all of a sudden, Orion the Hunter, Cygnus the Swan and so on.

We literally connected the dots, made up stories and celebrated them.

This is the same with our dots, our individual moments.

Stanislav Grov in his book '*Realms of the Human Unconscious*' refers to the Coex (Condense Experiences) constellations.
Although his book, and work in this space, is very much about serious mental trauma (not a read for the faint hearted) and how when not fully dealt with the patterns will recycle and repeat themselves and when mapped become like a constellation.

The positive is also true.

We can map our stories across the years, a collection of dots connected to create our own constellation. Like the stories we tell about the stars.

Robert Moore in his recorded lectures for 'The King Within' uses the verb in relation to connecting ourselves internally and externally to a source of energy and a thinking that drives a more positive interaction with the world.

Rather than shying away from a greater version of ourselves, engaging it and tapping into it by connecting these dots internally first. "To constellate the King within..."

When we do this for ourselves and our own moments, we can draw upon the meaning we find in this analyse, we can create a physical and visible representation of us, at our best and in doing so attract and stimulate the brain in new ways to review and absorb what happened.

Then help ourselves to elevate our own game moving forward through this experience.

"HE NEVER WITHDRAWS FROM IT. HE DOESN'T "THINK TOO MUCH," BECAUSE THINKING TOO MUCH CAN LEAD TO DOUBT, AND DOUBT TO HESITATION, AND HESITATION TO INACTION"

- ROBERT MOORE

Action -

Rate each story on a -10 to +10 continuum.

-10 is the *"negative"* +10 being the *"positive"*

Map every story on your time line, rate each one in the strength of impact on you.

Make a dot at the right level of strength across the sliding scale of -10/+10 and title each dot on your time line.

Once this is done, you'll need to find the strongest ones. Get all your 9's and 10' the highs and lows and see how many you have. You need around 5-8 stories in total at the end of this exercise.

These happenings are the core of your analysis the more challenging, the more extreme the better.

Why? Because in these events as the saying goes *"you don't rise to the expectation you fall back to the level of training"*

We cannot pretend in these moments; we just do us.

Get all your titles and dots on your sheet. Chronological order.

Connect your dots.

-10

0

+10

NOW

DETAIL

Now we're starting to build a clearer understanding.

Having gone through each of these processes myself I know there are already some glimmers of information. Some bits that are starting to stand out.

There may have been some tears already, some excitement and some sadness.

The further we dive into this, the more interesting it becomes. We have to ask ourselves some curated questions to get the depth in this dive.

Yes, the emotions will come up, it's inevitable, I'll say it again we're human, we're emotional beings learning how to experience ourselves in this reality. In mapping this through we are starting to scratch another layer of detail and the true reward comes from the digging that follows the scratching.

When I was heading down this road and had got to this point in my revelations, it was recommended several times to get a coach or sounding board that could help to ask me the right questions. It took ages to find any one, let alone the right one.

Like myself at the beginning of my coaching journey, every one I asked, honestly, was not ready themselves. I was wanting to get clarity on my driving nature, my inspiration and get into some of my 'stuff'.

Looking back, I realise that when we help others do their work it helps us to do ours. And, if they're not ready, they'll say no to helping you because it means putting a spot light on themselves.

I bounced from one person to the next, ending up with large pauses between conversations.

It took me some time to bring it together. It was, however, in the pauses that new ideas did filter up to the surface of my awareness.

With a coach or set of questions this can happen more succinctly, directly and much, much faster.

For me it took nearly 18 months to bring this all together. But that was purely because I was out there, in the majority, on my own.

HOW TO GET THE DETAILS

It's all about the questions we ask ourselves.

If we want to understand something we have to investigate, enquire and get curious and as Walt Whitman said

"BE CURIOUS, NOT JUDGMENTAL"

Remember this as you start to lift the lid on things;

You did the best you could with the best you had, just like your mum and dad did earlier in this book.

You did what you knew at the moment. Doesn't make it right or wrong just makes it what it was and, as always, hind sight is always 20/20. Easy to give yourself a hard time with a new set of understandings on an event and that is definitely not what we're here for. We want knowledge, insight and a deeper comprehension.

And you can't get that when your judging yourself.

Action -

Get your time line in front of you, the one with the constellations of life events on it.

Find a fresh A4 page with nothing on the back and write the title of the first story you want to work on at the top. The first story with the highest scoring. Remember 9's or 10's.

Here's your questions to work through on this sheet and, ideally, we want to keep it to 1 sheet.

- What happened?
- What was your part?
- What did you, or wish you did, contribute?
- What did, or do you wish, someone did for you in this event?
- What emotions came up?
- What valuable lessons did you learn?
- What was the result of the learning and/or the contribution that was made by you?
- What was the gift in all this?
- What have you repeated since then?

As we complete these questions, we're looking for verbs, contribution, actions. We're looking for the things you did that made the event come to life emotionally for you.

Ie. Carry, lift, guide, coach, inspire, mentor, teach.

You're looking for positive contribution to the event.

For the last four questions we're looking for impact, we're wanting to understand the growth of yourself or the other people involved as a result of the contribution.

Here's an example from my stories; one I've shared here previously and it's about being Bullied.

What happened? *Bullied each day on the way home from school.*

What was your part? *Walking home confronted by several older boys, was deeply intimidated and either put up with the abuse or ran away. I played victim.*

What did you, or wish you did, contribute? *I did a lot of scared, a lot of running and hiding from others and myself. Rather than stepping up to the challenge I played small. I was afraid and rather than seek help I stayed scared and didn't push myself.*

What did, or do you wish, someone did for you in this event? *I wish someone had been with me, or challenged me to set some boundaries, or tell me it's ok to ask for help when I needed it, I ran away from what I was actually capable of.*

What emotions came up? *Fear and resentment.*

What valuable lessons did you learn? *Later on, I learned Hurt people hurt people, I learned that I could also hurt people from not understanding my pains. I learned that I didn't want to let other people do this and wanted to challenge this perceived norm that happens in schools and in the work place, because it's not ok.*

What was the result of the learning and/or the contribution that was made by you? *Then I became a bully.* Now, I understand why people do this and can see both sides of the equation.

What was the gift in all this? *I got bigger and stronger and can now share this with others to help reshape the world.*

What have you repeated since then? *I've looked for the challenges; positive of negative I've always tried to challenge myself and others to push themselves and their boundaries.*

In the above example look for the verbs, look for the emotions, look for the growth opportunities in this.

Challenge – comes up a lot.
Understanding – seeking my own and others understanding.
Getting stronger – I became stronger and now I help other people do the same.

And these elements come up time and time again for me.

Action -

Now look at your stories. Take one sheet per event you wish to review. Write your answers on one side.

Don't use the back of the paper just one side and work through each scenario with these questions.

"THE ERROR OF THE PAST IS THE WISDOM AND SUCCESS OF THE FUTURE."

DALE TURNER -

BUILDING YOUR PURPOSE STATEMENT

BRING IT TO 1 SHEET

CONTRIBUTION -

Get all your sheets in one place, on a large table or flat surface.
Look at the events and find out what it was you were doing and list the actions. Again, linking the language back to the Day 0 responses, looking through all the stories that have played out and been recorded here.

1 way to do this is to put all the sheets on the floor and stand up to literally get an over view. Step back from the table and see everything in front of you.

Pick out the repeated words, the verbs that create emotional significance and meaning to them.

Action -

Take a different coloured pen, maybe a green, and start circling the words or phrases that repeat themselves.

Start tallying and keep score of the words that keep coming up, you will start to see a correlation between your 'star' moments.
List them on a fresh page.

Look for similar words that mean the same thing, start to get sight of the thing you do; consistently. Consciously or unconsciously.

Take a fresh A4 sheet of paper, divide the page up. Create 4 columns and 4 rows.

Consolidate and stack the repeated values and actions you've circled; compile a list of behaviours and activities you include as you at your best. These will include passed times, hobbies, elements of your job you truly love. It will also be core behaviours you demonstrate time and time again.

Challenging, Coaching, Supporting, Guiding, Harnessing, Stabilising.

This then starts your 'Inventory of Incredible'. Which comes up on Pg 200.

Here's a list of more examples you can pull in....

Growing, Delivering, Triangulating, Celebrating, Collaborating, Developing and Communicating

GROWTH -

You will also have a list of impacts you created in those stories; outcomes of the contributions you made. You can start to see trackable connections from the activity to the impact to the feelings they generate.

We can see where the sensations come from in relation to an action we've taken.

From this we can see how we can calculatedly, cultivate this in our future planning and steps.

Action -

On a separate sheet to the Values and Actions, create a new list in the same format for your Impacts and outcomes. The physical, tangible developmental leaps of those you gave to in those moments. This demonstrates action and reaction.

THE FIRST DRAFT

You will now have 2 lists – actions and contributions, impacts and growth. All of which retrieved from seeing what you inherited from Mum or Dad.

Also, from your Day Zero stories, how you've impacted others and how you've enriched their lives as a result of the things you did for them over the course of your life so far.

Common words that are the most significant to you – that are full of Meaning and at the same time full of Purpose because of what they've delivered for others.

These are the words that need to be harnessed and directed. This will make a large part of your first draft, a way to bring the focus in, like working a pair of binoculars or a microscope. We start at one point and then focus in steadily to bring the clarity and to strengthen the view.

Remember –

I am … [*action/contribution*]
So That … [*impact/growth*]

Right now, it is not about perfection and as Tony Robbins says *"Perfection is the lowest level of attainment, because it doesn't exist."* It's about starting to focus in on, expand, and strengthen it.

Bring it first to your attention through the earlier exercises and start bringing an element of deliberacy in to it.

Action -

Step 1. Make your first draft –

I am – [*fill in the blanks/insert the verbs*]
So that – [*fill in the blanks/insert the impacts you create*]

Initially when I worked through this process my 'Purpose' Statement was –

"*I am challenging people so that they can be better than yesterday*"

Get the words down so that you have a working version, immediately. Contribution then Growth. Even if you take no further action from here, it already creates a focal point for you to work with.

Step 2. Read it out loud to yourself –

How does it feel? And I mean physically, what emotions come up and do you feel it resonate at a physical level when you say it?

For me, the first statement I wrote felt like it was in the right space, definitely wasn't ticking enough boxes, emotionally.

It simply didn't feel strong enough, not enough punch to it. Didn't match what I was doing when I was firing on all cylinders, that goose bumps reaction when working with my clients.

One way to check in on this - If you were to live by that statement for the rest of your life would that be substantial enough for you? Or, is there a higher version of it and of you to be living in and up to?

Step 3. Review -

What words can you change about?

Do the words need to be changed and swap about?

Clients I have worked with on their statements felt some of the words around the contribution and the impact were in the wrong places. Upon reading them, they've promptly rubbed words out and swapped them around.

Always keep you inventory to one side so you can come back to it throughout the process. At each amendment they have re-read the new Purpose Statement – back to Step 2 to check in.

Mine developed up to – *"I am challenging peoples thinking so that they can become more incredible than yesterday"*

Still feeling like there were elements missing I had to review again. Firstly, I found that *"better than yesterday"* just wasn't meaty enough for me. I'm here to deliver something far bigger than that.

Secondly, there are impacts of my work that, for me, had to be included and vocalised – now, for some shorter is better, less wordy demonstrates their personality more succinctly. For me there are some extra layers to include.

I went back and found what the other parts are that I create and deliver when working at my best.

Step 4. Test it again -

Add the stronger words, move the language around find the strongest output, the articulation that makes you sit up and stand up in what you do and take notice of yourself.

This will take time – it's not an immediate result it often takes several attempts and repetition. Keep adjusting it a notch at a time and also start getting use to sharing it with others.

Even 5 years after starting this process I have had to adjust it. The language I was using was starting to become detrimental to me.

'Challenge' in my purpose is a fixed element, how I focus it though is down to me. How do you think my life is if I continually seek to challenge everyone and myself?

I've now added some positivity into it – '*I am positively challenging....*'

This makes my interactions much smoother as I bring this into my thinking.

"I BELIEVE THAT ALL OF US ARE BORN UNIQUE, BUT MOST OF US DIE COPIES."

- LES BROWN

Step 5. Start saying it to people -

See what the responses are. First test it on your friends, see how they respond and react when you share it with them – get their feedback.

Take time to ask them how they feel when you say this is what you're looking to bring in the future or you've delivered previously. See what they say.

I've had plenty of time to practice my 'Purpose' statement. When people ask me now what I do I tell them "I *help people become more incredible than yesterday*".

When I lead a training session, or introduce a coaching conversation I say to people "I *am going to positively challenge your thinking so that...*"

Peoples responses and reactions will quickly tell you how engaged they will be and whether they want to know or experience more of it.

Step 6. Build, improve, repeat and review -

Remember it's not about what you hope to be, it's what you already are.

Keep testing it until you have something that rolls off the tongue and enables you to engage very swiftly with the task at hand and resets your mindset immediately.

This is why I start my training and coaching sessions with this. Primes the mind for the interaction ahead.

WHAT IS AN INVENTORY OF INCREDIBLE?

It's a set of skills and attributes you'd class as your emotional, intellectual and/or physical specialities.

Much like a real time, real life version of some elaborate computer game – each person having specific skills related to their chosen role or character class.

The Thief type character being able to climb ropes and picks locks, the Magician able to conjure fire and absorb huge amounts of information.

This is the start of your specific and personal drop-down menu of powers and attributes.

The inventory works very similarly to a gap analysis, primarily though this is about you and the things you do that create the best possible outcomes.

See the illustration on page [x]
We break this down into 3 rows;

Skills
Knowledge
Behaviours

And we list out all the things we do on a daily basis, with family, at work or in our spare time.

List out all the things you do from the previous exercises. Then score them 1-10. 1 being poor, 10 being incredible.
Normally, in more traditional gap analysis for workplace personal development plan, we now measure the distance between the graded ability and 10.

Eg. I put down coaching as a skill and rate this as a 6. The distance between this and 10 is 4.

4 (the rating of the gap) is the number we score against to see what we want to work on.

And, again traditionally at this point most coaches and leaders would start looking for ways to bridge the biggest gaps.

What are the largest gaps and how do we improve them? I'm not a proponent of this, in simply attempting to raise every one's weaknesses we end up with a bunch of average.

There's a reason why they're weaknesses and by doing this we're encouraging mediocrity.

Look, unless you truly need to work on them – don't. The reason it's probably that low is because it isn't interesting therefore, you'll have little to zero interest in actually improving it any way.

In this frame work we add another column 'Excitement' again we grade this 1-10, same scale.

The piece of information we want to retrieve is where we are 9's and 10's in ability and 9' and 10's in excitement.

We add the 2 scores together and the closer we get to 20 – these are the one we work on.

This is a much clearer indication of internal desire and inspiration to do something and create traction on things.

Vishan Lakhani talked about strong strengths and strong weaknesses. We maybe phenomenal at spreadsheets in Excel, but hate doing it.

The problem is people see we're good at something and automatically assume we enjoy it.

The issue and frustration with this, people will give you more of this work due to their wrong assumption. Simply breeding more unhappiness in your current role.

Finding our strong strengths helps us to isolate that which truly drives us, internally. By also getting a view point on our strong weaknesses we can also start to say "No" to a few more things or start delegating a bit more.

The next benefit to this is when we find things, we're really good at and are truly inspired to do, we will take those 9's and 10's and make them 11's and 12's.

We will become specialists in our space and start to push the proverbial envelop to help shape the craft moving forward

"IF THERE'S SOMETHING I DON'T LIKE ABOUT ANYTHING, I DO NOT BITCH ABOUT IT, I CHANGE IT."

— VISHEN LAKHIANI

Exercise -

List out your skills, values, knowledges, actions you take in your work or home life.

Combine these with what you've already discovered through this book then get them all in one list broken down by;

- **Skill**
- **Knowledge**
- **Behaviour**

Then benchmark them all in the second column in relation to where you think you are on that 1-10 scale.

Then score them again in the third column for excitement 1-10 Add the 2 values together – how close is this to 20?

Now you can see what you're good and great at and also what actually excites you.

Then in the final column you can start to add some actions in there on how you would like to develop these aspects further with new learning, classes, online courses or books.

NB. This list will change over time. Like your taste buds as you get older certain foods will become less palatable. It's the same with the work we do, certain jobs and tasks become less appealing and that's ok. This just means it's time to move on from that task and either automate it or delegate it. By doing this exercise regularly it will help you stop tasks from getting stall long before you become really agitated by it and get the support you need from someone that either is just starting to find a passion in it or still finds it interesting or fascinating and would gladly take the work off you.

INVENTORY OF INCREDIBLE

Descriptors	Benchmark	Gap	Excitement	Next Steps
Skills				
Knowledge				
Behaviours				

HOW TO ADD MORE DEPTH TO THIS

Although we can draw great realisations and extract the core language we use from these concepts, these are not the only ways.

We can also analyse our environment and what we consciously and unconsciously surround ourselves with. We leave ourselves numerous physical clues as to what is of highest value and regard to us.

What we do though is accumulate things and people and experiences. Yet because these things build up over a course of time, we don't necessarily see the common thread running through these things so clearly. We don't reconcile our outer world as the reflection of our inner world.

Again, taking the time to question these things gives us a deeper understanding of ourselves. We create our world based on who we are, we put pieces of art in it which represent sentiments and emotions. We associate with people that help us to demonstrate certain behaviours for them positively or negatively. Much like seeing your own child grow and develop you don't see the changes because they're so gradual and until you take time to look at old photo's you're suddenly floored by how far they've come.

Stop and take a look around you;

- What is important to you right now?
- What have you surrounded yourself with, and who?
- What is it they're encouraging you to bring to the front of your thinking?
- And if you've stopped noticing them, what did they encourage when you put them there?

Exercise -

At the end of every Purpose discovery with my clients I've included a series of emails that helps to embed the thinking.

It's a series of prompts to nudge and gentle guide the thinking in order to keep it moving in the right direction, this is about holding the new understanding centre stage and to maintain alignment.

With the new calibration and insight these questions will suddenly inspire new outcomes. They'll help to demonstrate what it is that is most important to you and help advertise and indicate what truly matters; to you.

Before getting into this activity, this section can be a little 'chicken and egg.' We can use the responses to this as much to add to our 'Inventory of Incredible' and help build our 'Purpose Statement' as much to use the answers to strengthen the language we found in our research.

Follow each of these points, see what comes up and find out how this adds to the thinking and helps you clarify further.

On the other side, if you have got a statement see how this strengthens this for you physically and see what comes up;

"PROGRESS IS IMPOSSIBLE WITHOUT CHANGE, AND THOSE WHO CANNOT CHANGE THEIR MINDS CANNOT CHANGE ANYTHING."

- GEORGE BERNARD SHAW

6-PROMPTS

1. Space -

What can you introduce to your space that would remind you every day of who you are?

Not only do I have a multitude of house plants and incredible developmental literature I also have some reminders.

From images of my direct family; my wife and daughter to remind me who I bring when I'm at my best and who I want to be in relation to them. I also have representations of influential people and characters real and imagined;

Bruce Lee – a man of incredible fortitude, discipline and character.

Gandalf – A sage, a wizard immensely compassionate and wise.

Yoda - A leader of unbreakable faith in the order of things and natural power.

I also have Samurai and octopi that represent a way of thinking and approaching challenges.

They all remind me what I'm capable of when I activate my thinking and feelings.

They also give me a focal point for my thinking whenever I'm stuck; "*What would Gandalf do right now?*"

Because of the way our brain is wired, it will automatically create an answer. Yes, even from a make-believe mentor residing in Middle Earth.

Action -

Think about what it is you have in your space right now. What is inspiring you and encouraging you and, vice versa, what is detracting from this?

Establish what you can put in that helps you raise your game and start including it.

Find physical representations to include that give you that physical, mental and emotion stimulus.

- Pictures/Places
- Role models/Figures
- Reminders/Quotes/Memes

"TO KNOW ONESELF IS TO STUDY ONESELF IN ACTION WITH ANOTHER PERSON."

- BRUCE LEE

2. Time and Energy -

How are you concentrating your time and energy?

Realign your day by reconciling what you spend time and energy on. What are you dedicating yourself to and how does that truly demonstrate you at your best?

Get clear, as Tony Robbins said *"Where your focus goes, energy flows"*

Understanding our purpose and the things that truly light us up makes it much easier to find more of those things to brighten it further. It's not rocket science. If something detracts, find ways to delegate that to others that enjoy it.

If it makes us smile and we want to dedicate time and energy to it, find ways to spend more than 80% of your day doing those things.

Action –

Break down what you do on a daily basis.

Start with your work activities. Home life is a bit different, sometimes we do things we don't enjoy because it makes our respective partners happy and that strengthens the relationship.

At work, we relate to many people and that enjoyment varies due expertise and enjoyments. Why deprive someone else of something they find enjoyable by doing something that makes your miserable?

3 columns –

Hate / Neutral / Love

List out all of your daily activities across these 3 columns.

Column 1 - 'Hate'

Put everything you 'Hate' in here; draining, detracting and subtracting from you at your best. You've either evolved passed it some time ago or cannot understand why the business still does this thing. Because you've evolved passed this, it simply breaks your spirit to keep doing it.

Column 2 – 'Neutral'

This is just time filling and repetitive. Un inspiring and un–requiring of thought or problem solving.

Neither of these first 2 columns challenge you or push you. You've either learned them to a satisfactory level and have no want or need to take them further or have evolved beyond them. In both cases it's time to delegate them to people that either need to learn this as part of their job or development or seek an AI alternative to take this over so you can get on with the stuff that Spark Joy as Marie Kondo puts it.

"DO WHAT YOU LOVE AND THE NECESSARY RESOURCES WILL FOLLOW."

- PETER MCWILLIAMS

Column 3 - 'Love'

The final column is the stuff you want to find ways to do more of, however that maybe. It's the Meaningful and the Purposeful space of activity.

The idea is to train up someone to do the things in column 1 and 2 so you don't have to. Find people whose column 3 can be filled with your 1's and 2's. Get them to take that part of your job so you can get promoted to do the stuff in this column more of the time.

Create business projects that encourage these activities to happen.

Better still, find a way to open a business that does this 'stuff' on a massive scale, all of the time and help millions of people. Not only do you spend time doing work you love, you focus it on helping humanity.

Win-Win.

"EVERYONE HAS BEEN MADE FOR SOME PARTICULAR WORK, AND THE DESIRE FOR THAT WORK HAS BEEN PUT IN EVERY HEART."

RUMI -

3. Money –

How do you spend your money?

What are you channelling your resources into on a regular basis? Where are you diverting funds from and to?

Are you buying books and training material that develop aspects of your thinking and approach? Do they encourage how you approach life?

We have to expand and grow and develop.

Life requires that so we can continue to increase our impact and outputs.

Oak trees don't stay the same size? No, they pack on weight and mass and create more acorns. They become home for *more* creatures and produce *more* oxygen. They don't just fold up their leaves and close shop when they get bored.

Action –

Review how you're applying your resources and how this is developing you, your family and your professional life.
What is lifting you up or holding you down?
What books did you buy, what money did you squander?

Not judging, just reporting – document it.

What's important and what activities would make it more complementary to your new thinking?

Using the lens of purpose and the language that is resonating with you how else would you like to direct this resource?

4. Disciplined and organised -

Where are you most disciplined, organized and reliable?

These answers will again give you real clues about what you hold in high regard, and also what is the vehicle that helps you to embody you purpose.

For me, my Purpose being about challenging peoples thinking comes out in several key areas; Martial Arts, Gardening and Coaching.

Although these are varied subjects, I still channel my Purpose through them.

These three spaces are where I am most organised and energised. I get disciplined and schedule because I want them to be right, I want them to be seen as my area of expertise as my best foot forward.

When you start to review what aspects enable your truest contribution you can start to focus even further into these and lift them up.

Actions –

Write down the top three things that truly light you up, that invoke military precision in your work, that no one has to remind you to take action on, ever.

Take the time to review these activities and then see how your Purpose comes to life through these.

5. Thinking -

What dominates your thoughts?

What do you talk to yourself about most and what do you talk to others about most?

When you go home at the end of the day what thoughts come up for you most? What conversations bother you and what's the reason for that? What was important about them to you?

Was there a conversation that went badly and wish you would've done something different? Would you plan to correct it tomorrow?

What is the thing you remind yourself to do more of on a daily basis to best represent you in every moment?

And finally, what's that thing you love talking about, and worry that others will get bored of hearing about if you keep on about it?

The reason you worry, think and talk about these things is because you love them. That's not something to shy away from that's something to encourage in yourself. You cannot dim someone else's light by shining brighter. It's impossible. When we shine, we encourage others to shine.

As long as we do it to help them shine, we're in the best place.

"THOUSANDS OF CANDLES CAN BE LIT FROM A SINGLE CANDLE, AND THE LIFE OF THE SINGLE CANDLE WILL NOT BE SHORTENED. HAPPINESS NEVER DECREASES BY BEING SHARED."
— THE TEACHING OF BUDDHA

Action –

Imagine you've just been asked to go to a meeting with the senior managers because you're the expert. They want your opinion to help redirect the business and create lasting impact.

What are they asking you to share that is most important to you and why you?

What characteristics is it that made them ask for you?

"VISION IS THE ART OF SEEING WHAT IS INVISIBLE TO OTHERS." - JONATHAN SWIFT

6. Vision –

What is it you see and dream about in your life and what has already started to present itself to you?

Vision is only one thing; it's cerebral. It requires emotional thought to drive the engine that makes it happen. When we apply the emotion though and the action starts to happen, people start to see what it is we're creating and through our contribution things start to appear.

Action –

How is your vision being articulated, aligned to and strengthening your Purpose?

Again, use these answers to contribute to the language of you. What's important to you when you see the grandest version of you playing your greatest game, delivering your most magnificent accomplishments?

CLARIFYING YOUR PURPOSE

If your Purpose isn't clear there will be more in these 6 answers to retrieve, include and share. Find the answers that interlink, have similar words or repeat.

Again, a super clue indication of the parts that can be included or focused on to continue that cultivation of feeling, contribution and impact.

If the Purpose is clear, these answers can be used to flesh the vision out further and help you keep the thinking focused and ideas and on track.

Use the response to start filling your physical space with the things that remind you who you are.

Use the realisations to start building new relationships with those that challenge you to be the highest version of you more often.

Use the answers to start drilling down into the right books and content to up elevate your thinking in alignment to who you are and where your journey is going.

By doing this, all future moments will be given an extra boost and keep lifting you and your journey.

These are the elements, and the evidence, that you're on the right road and will keep you on the path as you progress.
Remember your successes (even the things you think aren't successes) left you clue's, your repeated behaviours are analysable. Your repeated and repeatable behaviours are what you're looking for. Not someone else's expectations.

Action –

Get more of these elements into your Inventory, add your values into the behaviours.

See where the cross overs are and find the repetition.

To expand this, probe to see how you rate yourself in your expression of these behaviours. Again 1-10 in each element. Use the analysis to find and see new ways to build them and express them more fully or clearly.

Review your levels of skill and excitement in each of these, which ones mean the most to you and also in what environments do they mean the most to you?

When you can see this, again physically in your own handwriting you can start think about how else you can you make use of your values and deepen your levels of fulfilment and eliminate the negative sentiments, especially in our work.

Because knowing our values in this way, on their own, is immensely powerful. With or without an 'I am' statement.

This is a huge part of our moral compass, the internal guidance system that moves us towards and away from what we see as beneficial or painful.

Brought together and included in the Inventory and combined with the analysis of our behaviours the values gain even further strength and credibility.

Imagine yourself as a company, an organisation or business of sorts.

VALUES AND WORK

Every great company has a set of guiding principles.

Their values.

Something that creates and directs behaviour to help those working inside the business deliver the best possible results for the company and aligned to the mission or vision.

Why are they important and why do they make such a difference inside business?

Reading 'Gallup's Approach to Culture' they highlighted;

"A values-driven culture can fuel organizational growth and attract top talent. Talented people want to work for an organization with a thriving culture.

In turn, employees who belong to fulfilling workplaces are more likely to serve as brand ambassadors who recruit talent and deliver compelling customer experiences."

Yet, as individuals, we either never get taught how knowing our own values is important or fail to realise how they give us momentum.

Convert the above statement to yourself;

"A values-driven individual can fuel their own growth and attract top talent. Talented people want to work with, and for, an individual with a mission to create a thriving culture.

In turn, an individual who has this internal driver and level of fulfilment is more likely to serve as their own brand ambassador and attract talent and deliver a compelling people focused experience."

It works for business as well as for us. Be your own brand and business.

Often organisations illustrate words on walls and encourage people to be Brave or Vulnerable or Bold. Getting them on the wall is absolutely right but these businesses miss the prime element of the whole activity; how we actually embody these concepts, how we actually breathe life into these thoughts through action.

What are the activities that make this real?

By asking the previous questions first, reviewing your environment, you're thinking and the actions you take throughout each day of your life, you can already see the activities that are born from the values and then, do more of it.

By knowing them and the associated activities you can keep these up-front in your daily habits and routines because you already know what you want to create more of in the world around you. We can start to plan goals and action steps based on our Values and inspirations, it can help us to align our job applications, career decisions into the future and guide our developmental decisions around our education and leadership skills.

For those job seeking or looking at promotions knowing your own values helps you to apply with companies that embody what you hold dear. We start to find good fits for who we are by using the values as the lens.

For those building careers and looking at new career paths, it helps us to think about what sort of job titles and skills will help us to deliver more of our values.

For the leaders of people and entrepreneurs it helps us to set the tone of the team and environment we want to create.

When we're clear who we are, we can place ourselves in the best possible space and encourage the best possible people to work with us.

That starts internally; me knowing me.

What do I bring? And, equally important, how does this space facilitate me bringing more of it?

We don't put cacti in a freezer. We know what they prefer, so we find the right place and relocate them so they can flourish and grow.

We know what's important to them so we put them in the best possible surroundings.

Even with a rough rule of thumb on your own preferences, you can make better decisions about where you want and intend to be on a daily basis.

You can start deciding where you'd like to be in order to thrive.

You can choose the environment you'd like to define.

And surprisingly, at an organisational level very few people strongly agree with their company's values; again. According to Gallup only 27% strongly agree in fact. And yet again, line this up with the lack of engagement in the work and then with the levels of anxiety found at work.

Knowing yourself is vital.

Knowing your values helps develop Meaningful work.

Knowing what creates joy in your world and that of others builds Purposeful work.

One feeds the other and in turn leads into the next and however we approach this, when we start using any of these tools shared in this book, we can start building and magnifying the fulfilment in every one of our days moving forward.

Which keeps us looping back into and building more Purposeful work day in and day out.

"YOUR BELIEFS BECOME YOUR THOUGHTS, YOUR THOUGHTS BECOME YOUR WORDS, YOUR WORDS BECOME YOUR ACTIONS, YOUR ACTIONS BECOME YOUR HABITS, YOUR HABITS BECOME YOUR VALUES, YOUR VALUES BECOME YOUR DESTINY."

GANDHI -

https://www.gallup.com/workplace/243434/time-core-values-audit.aspx

MAKING USE OF 'YOUR' PURPOSE

This book is truly the art and science of finding purpose. The methodology to start isolating your language, it is the initiating steps to become fluent in this way of speaking. Your way of speaking, and as a result start recalibrating your behaviours and actions before you even instigate them.

Although the consistent golden thread of philosophy will run through everything you do, you have to remember this will be a constant work in progress. Refining and refocusing your actions on a daily, hourly and minutely basis to the thing which is you at your core.

Once we have this golden thread, the golden truth of you, then you can start to more clearly focus it in to manifesting your goals and building incredible habits to define that Day 0, that death bed celebration. It's about constantly reminding and habitualising it through repetition and monitoring the impacts of doing what you do that is of Purpose.

This is a proven method to increase the impact you bring through the understanding of how you actually work; neurologically, physically, emotionally and genetically.

By doing this you can start to consciously choose what it is you want to bring and how you will show up every amazing day, start breaking old habits, even when it's someone else's habits you've learned.

This is the way, your way to start connecting your dots moving forward, the ability to throw yourself into your future and elevate the outcome.

"Begin with the end in mind" he said.

By knowing this, your purpose, the end is always in mind because you action at the start will be a reflection of who you are when you're at your best – consciously, congruently and calculatedly.

This is how you predict the future as Abraham Lincoln suggested – by creating it, by knowing the actions that you're putting in to start with that develop an end you will be proud of and hand on heart elated about.

That's the difference.

HOW TO MAKE IT WORK

Get yourself, and be, super aware of this language – it isn't hard. Just have to use it regularly. What it does require is; routine. It needs to be constantly reviewed, maintained and homed in on. This is something I cover in more depth in Book 3 – 'Legacy', practicing a daily review.

One of the founding thoughts I'll share here, one that will already start you moving forward.

"A ROCKET WON'T FLY UNLESS SOMEBODY LIGHTS THE FUSE!"

- HOMER HICKAM

Action -

At the beginning of each day as part of our morning routine, we need to review our day ahead;

Take the time each morning to sit in silence, after your meditation or Ideation if this is part of your practice and review your day ahead, set your day before you move into it.

The moment you start your day, it's already finished. This is the same for your week, your month, or year. The moment it begins it's already finished so we have to get super clear about what we're putting into it at the very beginning.

Start to clarify;

- What appointments do I have in my diary?
- What opportunities do have to connect with people?
- What conversations need to take place?

Once I can see my day, whether by looking at my diary, or just remembering the calendar, I think about the language of my Purpose statement. I focus on the core actions I talk about and take.

Have a look through the key verbs you have written down, what are they?

Mine is to challenge, expand peoples thinking, help them to become more incredible than yesterday.

I then take these key words and incorporate them into questions to focus my thinking.

As an example;

- What conversations will I be having today that I can positively challenge more peoples thinking?
- What meetings am I having which will enable me to expand people even further in their grandest versions?
- How can I help more people become more incredible than yesterday?

By doing this I'm already setting my intention for my day ahead; every action, every meeting, conversation and every activity.

Having aligned my day ahead with my own clear sense of purpose I can look to create bigger impacts at every possible juncture.

Even when the curve ball comes in.

Because I've already been practicing who I am at my best, it's easier for me to take the lead on that random event as it comes in. As it does, I still deliver an exceptional conversation that creates the impact I'm designed to.

Even on the fly.

"IN FACT, IT MAY BE NECESSARY TO ENCOUNTER THE DEFEATS, SO YOU CAN KNOW WHO YOU ARE, WHAT YOU CAN RISE FROM, AND HOW YOU CAN STILL COME OUT OF IT."

- MAYA ANGELOU

INTRODUCTIONS

The second way to start making it work for you; stop introducing yourself by job title.

Start introducing yourself by your Purpose.

"What do you do?"

The man asking me and smiled broadly as I replied;

"I help people become more incredible than yesterday"
"That sounds amazing, I could do with some of that" he replied.
To do this requires some practice, a bit of confidence and plenty of clarity on what your purpose is.

We have to be really comfortable with who we are when we're at our best, no questions and no doubts. Once you've delivered that first line and then, when they ask so how do you do that, you can then tell them about your 'job'.

The clearer you are on your Purpose, the easier these words roll off your tongue.

Practice and refine.

Refine -

You absolutely have to keep refining your Purpose statement until it feels right. Boil it down. Each time you
iterate and the closer you get to the truth the more confidence you'll express as you say it.

Practice -

As with everything we do, it will be clunky to start and as you start to really tap into and remember who you bring it will build its own momentum. With the energy gaining as you keep implementing.

It will start to feel natural.

It will begin to feel right.

It will be easy to say and it will attract people to you, drawn to the greatest version of your grandest self.

All qualified through your own reflection and verbalised through your own analyse.

"OUR TRUE PURPOSE IS REVEALED WHEN WE LET GO OF ALL THE IDEAS OF WHO WE THINK WE ARE."

KATE CHIFFEY GRAY -

WHAT HAVE WE COVERED?

- 4-Stages of work Taught, Told, Meaningful and Purposeful.
- A little Epigenetics and how far back the physical and neurological switches were being flicked on and off.
- Everything in nature, and existence, is a solution to a problem. Including you - you have a Purpose.
- How to move from 'Meaningful' to 'Purposeful'.
- How to start your 'Inventory of Incredible' and list out the actions you take when at your best.
- How to Structure your 'Purpose' Statement and have a first draft as a minimum.
- How to start using this statement directly to create impact no matter which draft you're on.

In short, knowing I had a purpose saved my life, finding out what it is has saved other peoples.

It's important. This is only the first step to build a huge wealth of fulfilment in your life.

Fulfilment comes from being full and being able to fill others.

Full/filling

I know this is true sitting here at the age of 41 rapidly heading towards 42 and looking back at my previous unstructured, unguided and unthought about life I see the absolute necessity to share this back with as many people as possible.

In whatever way I can.

If you want fulfilment start doing things for others. Start being deliberate in who you are when you're at your best.

This is where the good stuff is, the golden truth of where fulfilment is. Not in someone else's agenda, it's on your agenda, you doing you.

This book is the first pillar to structuring and creating fulfilment with consistency in your life, on a daily basis.

The second part comes with Goals.

It is the embodying and physical manifestation of your purpose.

You at your best and creating something in reality that demonstrates that purpose tangibly; the charity organisation, the business venture, the outcome of the activities you partake in.

It's the way you raise your family, stimulate those around you and things you want to build in honour of them.

Just take a moment to think what's possible when you're in the best of moods, think what you're capable of when your excited and proud to be part of a project or movement. Then amplify this by feeling like this nearly every day, if not every day.

When you start to hold this thinking at the front of your mind, it'll create the understanding of what is possible in 5 years, 20 years or even 100 years from now. Built upon you, living your truest self in every moment.

MY GOAL - 100 MILLION

I already know the impact of 1 person working with 1 person. I've had the pleasure of coaching others and seeing these individuals radically grow and develop through an elevation of thinking that has caused multiple promotions, increased sales and stimulated huge shifts in their personal lives.

What would happen if 100 million people changed gear at the same time, found their mountain and climbed it, upped their level and delivered a whole new range of impacts upon humanity?

How would civilisation shift? For me this book is a part of that shift, taking that 'if' to a 'when'.

A 'when' in my life time to power and level up 100 million people to live, create and be incredible.

100 million people thinking clearer, deliberately bigger and more impactfully.

What happens as a result? The plan, right now for me is to stop asking what the answer might be and make it an actually.
Making the dream a plan and take action on it.

By creating a next level, helping shape a progressive thinking that is so pervasive that incredible is a constant. That's where you join in.

1 of the 100 million voices getting heard, building your tribe, growing your people and creating fulfilment in your space.

And as you experience this, things will start to happen and when they do, I want to hear about them. Because when you share and someone else hears, you become the inspiration for them to go further. You become their virtual accountability. As you share, others learn, as they learn they grow and so on and so forth.

Relentless progression, at a new rate of development, with a new weight of momentum. Be the snow ball rolling down the hill, build the presence, build the people and build the outcome.

WHAT NOW?

How are you going to use the content of this book to help you find fulfilment in what you do right now?

What did you learn that is helping you to deliver stronger result in what you're applying yourself to in this moment?

What were the big take away learnings from this book for you this time round?

What did you learn along the way?

What did you, or will you share with other people?

Remember PAST learning – T is for Teach, compound your understanding by gifting it to someone else.

I love hearing what has happened or is happening for you as a result.

Drop me a message through LinkedIn.

As I said earlier in this book, it's not about jacking in the job, throwing it all in and cutting loose. It's about remembering why you do what you do, in any job and learning to enjoy it again so you can expand from it.

It's about re-sourcing that potential and that inspiration to go and do your version of incredible.

And also, this is only Book No.1.

Book 2 will cover 'Goals' with Book 3 covering daily habits that strengthen these and builds 'Legacy'.

These are the three needs of Fulfilment: Purpose, Goals and Legacy.

PURPOSE
GOALS
LEGACY =

FULFILMENT...

MAXIMISE THE VALUE

As you've read, much of this I've learned myself the hard way, picked up through experience and from various teachers. Some of those ideas I have expanded upon to create stronger results.

Throughout and where ever possible, if it is someone else's idea I have done my up most to credit them accordingly.

If you find that I have misquoted or miscredited someone then please email me directly and let me know so I can update this appropriately. It is hugely important to me to make sure this is right.

The true, and soul purpose of this document is to provide you with some key building blocks to keep shifting you forward by challenging your thinking so you can become more incredible than yesterday. That's all, I hope it has helped and will help.

I also want to make sure you get maximum value from this and any of my other materials, products, or services I offer and always want to multiply the value I'm adding.

Let me know what you think of this book. Your feedback all goes towards improving what I do for you, our community and future connections.

You get to give me your thoughts and help me become more incredible than yesterday!

Thanks in advance and enjoy the process.

BE INCREDIBLE

FINAL THANKS

Sarah Corbishley & Kevin Loss - Heart felt gratitude for pouring your time and attentions over this book in the ways that you have. For picking up as many of the typos, grammatical errors and complete nonsense I sometimes type.

Your care and dedication in helping get this into a format that is readable, understandable and digestible is truly, truly appreciated - Thank you.

For you reading this, you may still have found some - great.

I put enough in there to share around so you wouldn't feel left out.

Nathan Simmonds -

Leadership Coach, Trainer and Consultant

Everything I do is hinged on the premise of challenging people's thinking, so that they can take control of key elements in their lives, expand the greatest version of who they are and become more incredible than yesterday.

Physically, what I have done repeatedly is help leaders double their income or half their work week.

I help entrepreneurs and professionals cut through the noise of modern life, harness the stress and overwhelm to create clarity in the chaos.

Why?

So, they can create high quality time with most important people in their lives.

But, there's a lot of noise

A lot of overwhelm and

A lot of chaos.

If we don't take time to get the tools and skills to overcome this, move beyond it and do our version of incredible, we'll be swallowed up by it.

Printed in Great Britain
by Amazon